TENSIONS IN AMERICAN PURITANISM

PROBLEMS IN AMERICAN HISTORY

EDITOR

LOREN BARITZ

State University of New York, Albany

THE NATURE OF LINCOLN'S LEADERSHIP
Donald E. Fehrenbacher

THE AMERICAN CONSTITUTION
Paul Goodman

THE AMERICAN REVOLUTION
Richard J. Hooker

AMERICA IN THE COLD WAR
Walter LaFeber

ORIGINS OF THE COLD WAR, 1941–1947
Walter LaFeber

AMERICAN IMPERIALISM IN 1898
Richard H. Miller

TENSIONS IN AMERICAN PURITANISM
Richard Reinitz

THE GREAT AWAKENING
Darrett B. Rutman

WORLD WAR I AT HOME
David F. Trask

THE CRITICAL YEARS,
AMERICAN FOREIGN POLICY, 1793–1825
Patrick C. T. White

TENSIONS IN AMERICAN PURITANISM

EDITED BY

RICHARD REINITZ

JOHN WILEY & SONS, INC.

NEW YORK · LONDON · SYDNEY · TORONTO

10 9 8 7 6 5 4 3 2 1

Library of Congress Catalogue Card Number: 70-100325

Cloth: SBN 471 71560 3   Paper: SBN 471 71561 1

Printed in the United States of America

For my father
IRVING REINITZ

SERIES PREFACE

This series is an introduction to the most important problems in the writing and study of American history. Some of these problems have been the subject of debate and argument for a long time, although others only recently have been recognized as controversial. However, in every case, the student will find a vital topic, an understanding of which will deepen his knowledge of social change in America.

The scholars who introduce and edit the books in this series are teaching historians who have written history in the same general area as their individual books. Many of them are leading scholars in their fields, and all have done important work in the collective search for better historical understanding.

Because of the talent and the specialized knowledge of the individual editors, a rigid editorial format has not been imposed on them. For example, some of the editors believe that primary source material is necessary to their subjects. Some believe that their material should be arranged to show conflicting interpretations. Others have decided to use the selected materials as evidence for their own interpretations. The individual editors have been given the freedom to handle their books in the way that their own experience and knowledge indicate is best. The overall result is a series built up from the individual decisions of working scholars in the various fields, rather than one that conforms to a uniform editorial decision.

A common goal (rather than a shared technique) is the bridge of this series. There is always the desire to bring the reader as close to these problems as possible. One result of this objective is an emphasis of the nature and consequences of problems and events, with a de-emphasis of the more purely historiographical issues. The goal is to involve the student in the reality of crisis, the inevitability of ambiguity, and the excitement of finding a way through the historical maze.

Above all, this series is designed to show students how experienced historians read and reason. Although health is not contagious, intellectual engagement may be. If we show students something significant in a phrase or a passage that they otherwise may have missed, we will have accomplished part of our objective. When students see something that passed us by, then the process will have been made whole. This active and mutual involvement of editor and reader with a significant human problem will rescue the study of history from the smell and feel of dust.

Loren Baritz

ACKNOWLEDGMENTS

I wish to thank Loren Baritz, James Crenner, Melvin Hill, Michael McGiffert, and Gene Wise, all of whom read an early draft of my introduction article and made a number of valuable suggestions. Professor Baritz, the editor of this series, also provided much helpful advice about the materials to be included. Counsel offered has not always been taken and the ultimate responsibility is entirely my own.

Mrs. Rosemary Currie did an excellent typing job, and Stephanie Flather assisted with the proof reading.

A special thanks to my wife, Janet Reintz. Her patience, understanding and hard work have been essential to the production of this book.

A grant from the Hobart and William Smith Colleges Faculty Research Committee aided in the completion of the manuscript.

CONTENTS

INTRODUCTION   1

I. PIETY AND INTELLECT   17

    1. PERRY MILLER   17
       The Piety and the Federal Theology   17
       The Augustinian Strain of Piety   17
       The Covenant of Grace   25

    2. THOMAS HOOKER   38
       Human Sin and the Disruption of
       Divine Order   38

    3. THOMAS SHEPARD   47
       Salvation by Covenant   47

II. COMMUNITY VERSUS CALLING   53

    4. BERNARD BAILYN   55
       Puritan Social Ideals and the Dilemma of
       the New England Merchant   55

    5. JOHN ROBINSON   65
       Diligent labor and the use of Gods creatures   65
       Of Labour, and Idleness   66
       Of Callings   68
       Of the use, and abuse of things   71
       Of Riches, and Poverty   73

    6. JOHN WINTHROP   76
       A Modell of Christian Charity   76

III. LIBERTY VERSUS REFORMATION   87

        7. EDMUND S. MORGAN   89
            Roger Williams: The Church and the State
            The Intellectual Integrity of a
                Puritan Heretic   89
            The Business of Government   92
            Liberty of Conscience   96

        8. ROGER WILLIAMS   100
            The Bloudy Tenent   100
            The Demands of Truth   103
            The Integrity of Conscience   105

        9. JOHN COTTON   106
            The Bloudy Tenent, Washed   106
            Of the Magistrates Power   107
            Sinning Against One's Own Conscience 111

IV. THE BROTHERHOOD OF THE SAINTS VERSUS
     THE INNER LIGHT   113

       10. THE BOSTON FATHERS   115
            The Covenant of the First Church of
                Boston   115

       11. DARRETT B. RUTMAN   116
            Toward a New Jerusalem   116
            The Antinomian Controversy and Its
                Effects on the Boston Church   119

V. CHOSENNESS VERSUS UNIVERSALITY   133

       12. PERRY MILLER   135
            Errand Into the Wilderness   135

       13. EDWARD JOHNSON   154
            Wonder-Working Providence of Sions
                Saviour   154

14. ROGER WILLIAMS   157
    American Exceptionalism Rejected   157

VI. NEW APPROACHES   159

15. MICHAEL WALZER   161
    Puritan Repression and Modernization   161

16. SUMNER CHILTON POWELL   178
    The Origin and Stability of a New
        England Town   178

SUGGESTED READING   188

TENSIONS IN AMERICAN PURITANISM

INTRODUCTION

Puritanism was an English movement which became the single most influential factor in the shaping of American culture and society. An expression of the recurring need of men to confront their God directly, it demanded of its followers that they manifest their highly personal religious commitment in an active and effective public life. As a late thrust of the Reformation, Puritanism carried that great European upheaval into the American wilderness. It provided the process of colonization with a universal significance it would not otherwise have had and tapped sources of energy deeper than the economic and national motives that also propelled people across the Atlantic. A movement based on ancient Christian values, in the end it furthered the development of modern secular society. Aimed at the construction of a universal Protestant church, it became in its American form the rationale of a unique and highly distinctive people. Its outward thrust was intended to aid in the reformation of England, where it originated, but in the end it became the heart of a new culture.

The origins of Puritanism are complex and in part obscure. On the Continent the Reformation began as a religious movement but succeeded because it also became a political movement; in England it began as a political act but later took on meaning as a religious movement. Henry VIII, who simply wished to establish control over the church and to reap the economic and political benefits of the control, set forces in motion that extended well beyond anything he intended. Once the break with the Pope had been made, Protestantism followed.

Henry's death brought his minor son Edward VI to the throne under a regency in which men of deep Protestant persuasion held

1

power. They endeavored to move England farther along the road to reform, but Edward, short-lived, was succeeded by Mary Tudor, a Catholic, who returned the country to the Roman church. By this time there were many sincerely convinced Protestants in England, some of whom were burned for their faith, as Catholic martyrs had suffered under Henry VIII. Others, including many clergymen, fled to the centers of Protestantism on the Continent, particularly Geneva and the Rhineland, where they deepened their reformist commitments. Mary died in 1558 and Elizabeth I ascended the throne. Elizabeth, like Henry, was more interested in preserving the unity of the realm and the power of the Crown than in any particular religious position. She envisioned a church that would allow for a range of belief. Acceptance of the Crown as its head was the primary acknowledgment required. Those who remained deeply Catholic were excluded, as were those who would bypass the state in seeking greater reform.

It must not be assumed that worship and faith among the masses of the people followed all these twists and turns of the English establishment. The rural parishes of England had doubtless been affected by the changes, but not so deeply as one might think. Throughout our discussion of Puritanism it is important to remember that most of the people of England never became committed Puritans.

Puritanism as an identifiable movement, or set of movements, began under Elizabeth. It was the name, at first pejorative, given to those who sought further to purify worship and life. As it became clear that Elizabeth would go only so far, men with a deep belief in Protestantism became increasingly dissatisfied with the limited reformation of the Church of England. Prominent among them were the Marian exiles, those who had fled to Geneva or the Rhineland during Mary's reign.

Just what did these men mean by greater purity of life and worship? The specific content of Puritan goals varied among different reforming groups and changed to some extent in the course of the late sixteenth and early seventeenth centuries. In general, Puritans wanted a return to simpler forms of worship closer to those they felt were to be found in the New Testament.

They opposed an emphasis on the sacramental elements in religion, the wearing of vestments by the clergy, and ornate church decoration. They felt that Bible reading, listening to preaching, and self-examination ought to be the central religious activities. Puritans had a great concern with the inner spiritual life of the believer, although their intent was not to destroy all outward forms. In regard to church government they held a variety of different views. By the 1630's many Puritans were opposed to the bishops.

For the Puritans the worship of God was not confined to the church. All of life had religious significance and the reformation of society was divinely commanded. They sought to extend the power of the church over the behavior of the congregation, to increase church discipline. They were concerned to preserve the Sabbath for religious activities, and they opposed games of chance and frivolity in general on Sunday or any other day. To waste time and energy was sinful for they did not belong to man alone. It is most important to realize that the Puritans did not seek a monastic withdrawal from the world but rather an active participation in secular life, a participation with an eye toward the devine. Man must not avoid temptation. He must live with it and overcome it.

As the Puritans looked back to the primitive church for their ecclesiastical model, so in their social ideas they tended to return to an imaginary past. They perceived the manifestations of early capitalism around them as signs of social disintegration. Many men responded to such indications of change with feelings of insecurity, even of guilt. Most Puritans sought an ordered, hierarchical society as a means of allaying their inner discomfort.

Their differences with the established church were not primarily over matters of theology as such. Ideas of the nature of salvation were similar among Puritans and Anglicans, at least in the sixteenth century. Many men who shared some Puritan attitudes did not share others. Puritanism in the sixteenth century was as much a mood as a movement.

By the end of Elizabeth's reign distinctive groups began to appear among Puritans, although the lines dividing them were to take on sharper focus in the seventeenth century. The most

basic difference lay between separatists and nonseparatists. The
latter, by far the majority of Puritans, held that the Church of
England was to be regarded as a true church, but one of many
corruptions that ought to be cured from within. They would not
destroy the unity of religion by breaking with that church, for
religious unity was held to be essential to the integrity of society
itself. The separatists felt that the Church of England was corrupt
at its core, that it could not be reformed, and that true Protestants
must separate from it. In this they reasoned much as Anglicans
and Puritans in regard to the Church of Rome. The separatists
acted on their beliefs and established clandestine, illegal congregations in a few places in England and abroad. The Pilgrims
who settled Plymouth Colony belonged to a moderate faction of
separatists.

Even among the nonseparating majority of Puritans there
were divisions, based primarily on ideas of church government.
Some accepted the legitimacy of the rule of the bishops, although
by the middle of the seventeenth century, there were few Puritans
left who held that view. Most were Presbyterians who maintained that the church should be ruled by synods. Others were
Congregationalists who claimed to find in the New Testament a
pattern within which each congregation ruled itself according
to the word of God. The Congregationalists also held that
church membership should be restricted to the visible saints,
those who could reasonably be assumed to have received salvation. This was a logical prerequisite for their belief in independent church governments. If the congregation itself was to
rule, the only way all congregations could be expected to follow
the same policy (an aim that was not abandoned) would be if
all church members read the Bible with the divinely aided eyes
of the saved.

The separatists were Congregationalists in their view of church
government. Among them also were some of an even more
radical bent, successors of the Anabaptists of the sixteenth
century and precursors of the sects that were to appear during
the disruptions of the English Civil War.

The Puritans, who were forcefully evangelical, hoped to convert all of England by one method or another. Their major
center of influence was at Cambridge University, many of whose

students became clergymen and most of whom were touched by Puritan ideas and attitudes in the course of their education. The educated clergy as a group of disaffected intellectuals constituted in itself the social class most widely attracted to Puritanism, although by no means were all ministers converted by it.

As great as their influence was in some respects, the Puritans lacked the power to institute their reforms. The Queen was the head of the church as well as the state. At first it was hoped that if she could be brought to see the light, their light, she would lead their reformation. But Elizabeth was blind to the deeper sources of Puritan vision. When she died in 1603, there was for the moment the expectation that James I would lead them, but he proved to be unsympathetic to the cause.

As the Puritans became convinced that they were unable to convert the monarch, they turned more and more to Parliament for a sympathetic hearing. There was conflict between the House of Commons and the King over taxation and other matters in the early seventeenth century which paralleled the conflict between the Puritans and the King as the head of the church. Many members of Parliament were themselves Puritans or sympathetic to Puritanism. Many more recognized the common enemy: the royal prerogative in church and state.

When James died in 1625, his son Charles I, who was even more hostile to Puritanism than his father had been, succeeded to the throne. Under him, the Bishop of London, William Laud, later Archbishop of Canterbury, came to possess great power. Laud was determined to drive the Puritans from their positions within the church, and he largely succeeded in doing so.

At the same time the civil conflict between Crown and Parliament intensified. Charles was even more determined than his father had been to retain his royal prerogatives, and Parliament was increasingly anxious to assert its power. By 1629 their differences became so sharp that Charles prorogued Parliament and ruled England for eleven years without it.

The 1630's were a dark period for English Puritans. Their clergy were being dispossessed and frequently forced to flee the country. The hope of achieving reformation through Parliament was in abeyance, since that body did not meet for the entire decade. Under these conditions all that the Puritans in England could do was strengthen their lines and hope for a change.

Such a change was brought about by the Scots in 1640. A war with Scotland forced Charles to call a Parliament in order to raise taxes. The struggle between Charles and his Parliament soon escalated into a Civil War in which Puritans fought against Anglicans.

The conditions of this war also produced dissent among Puritans. The unity in opposition which the Puritans had sometimes demonstrated broke down with their hopes of seizing power, for the positive differences of belief in regard to church polity became more meaningful. The Presbyterian majority in Parliament (not in the country—most Englishmen were not on the Puritan side) called the Westminster Assembly to reform religion along Presbyterian lines, and the Congregationalists, now frequently called Independents, attempted to prevent the imposition of that reformation. In addition, a variety of more radical groups, called sects appeared once the restraints on pulpit and press were broken under the conditions of civil war. In order to protect themselves against the Presbyterians, the Congregationalists were forced to form an alliance with these sects and to accept the idea of limited religious toleration.

In the Civil War the Puritans were the victors, and the conflict within Puritanism was won by the Congregationalists because of their influence in the army led by Oliver Cromwell. Charles, after refusing serious compromise, was executed in 1649. Cromwell imposed a Puritan reformation on a largely hostile or indifferent English people,[1] but in a number of particulars it was quite different from the reformation expected by any Puritan of the 1620's or 1630's. For one thing, it created a degree of religious toleration.

Cromwell was unable to establish his government on any lasting foundation. By 1660 Charles's son was on the throne, and Puritanism in England turned into nonconformity. It had had its moment of power and failed, failed quite dramatically. It was burned out. Some Englishmen could still believe in Puritan principles, but they had lost the confidence that they were destined to impose them on the world.

Yet those principles had already been established in a new part of the world. Puritanism manifested itself within the complexities of Europe as a revolutionary movement; in America it became the ideological basis for a new society built on the hope of universal reformation.

In 1630, when the prospects for Puritanism had been bleakest, an offshoot had been sent to the New World. A group of Puritans who controlled the Massachusetts Bay Company decided that the most effective way to reform the Church of England would be to take a branch of it out of England to America. There it could be reshaped in Congregationalist terms; a model could be established for the reformation of England, and perhaps the world. They saw themselves as moving out from the center of their concern, not in withdrawal, but in anticipation of affecting the course of events at that center.

In New England, under the leadership of John Winthrop, they founded a group of towns and churches based on Puritan ideas. Their venture was an unusual experiment in the establishment of an intentional community. Within limits they had great independence because they had been able to take the charter for their colony with them. During the first fifteen years more than twenty thousand immigrants came to New England, the majority of whom were dedicated Puritans. The wilderness was cleared, churches built, and Puritan social and political institutions created. The pressures and opportunities of the American environment prevented those institutions, even in their beginnings, from being the perfect expression of the colonists' intentions, but those intentions were nonetheless amply visible in the colony.

The civil government of Massachusetts was developed out of the organizational structure of the chartered company that created the colony. Under the company rules the investors (known as "freemen"), meeting collectively as the General Court, elected an executive body composed of "assistants" who, in turn, chose the governor and deputy-governor. The major change introduced in transforming this corporate structure into the government of a colony was the extension of the rights of freemanship to all adult male church members in Massachusetts.

The colony contained a disproportionate number of highly educated clergymen who took the lead in forming the churches which, although nominally unseparated from the Church of England, were in fact practical applications of theories developed by Congregationalist theologians over many years. These churches were the heart of the community. The secular government, although formally distinct from the ecclesiastical structure, was dedicated to protecting the churches and to maintaining a godly community. Together the church and the state sought to foster an ordered, hierarchical society in which the individual effort to exploit the opportunities of America would be moderated by an ultimate devotion to God and a Christian concern for the good of the whole. Private morality was publicly regulated with particular care because of the collective responsibility of the community to carry out God's special mission for Massachusetts as the model for the reformation of the world.

The pattern of settlement adopted was one in which each of a number of small towns was centered around its own church. The area occupied by the Puritans spread rapidly. Villages were founded in the Connecticut River Valley, and good relations were established with Plymouth.

The New England Puritans welcomed the outbreak of the English Civil War as the moment for which they had been waiting. Their ultimate goal from the beginning had been the establishment of a model for the reformation of England. The success of their colony proved that Congregationalism could work. The turmoil in the mother country ought to lead to the adoption of their model. Because at first it appeared that the Presbyterians were dominant, most of the colonial clergymen who were invited to return to England refused to do so. Finally the English Congregationalists did come to power, but to the chargrin of the New Englanders their former allies now held different beliefs; a limited religious toleration was adopted and heretics similar to those exiled from New England were accepted in England. Cromwell did not attempt to impose his version of Congregationlism on the colonies. Massachusetts was left to continue in its own way, but whereas that way had once led in expectation to the center of the world it now led only toward the wilderness. The American Puritans continued to seek a universal destiny, but in fact New England had become irrelevant to all but itself and its American future.

That Puritanism in the New World did not weaken or collapse all at once when it became divorced from the mainstream of history is a great testament to its vitality. The religious commitment of New England remained deep and profound. Only gradually in the course of the second half of the seventeenth century did it sour. Within that century it never collapsed, but slowly it became both more conventional and more unsure of itself. Although Puritanism in England burned out and became a nonconformist thread in the fabric of later English life, in the New World it was transformed into a broad set of assumptions and habits that became the central pattern of American culture.

The lasting effects of Puritanism, the important role it played in English and American history and in the process of modernization, were products of its inner tensions. A religious movement based on a profound insight into the human condition, Puritanism was able to draw on new sources of energy and to apply them to a wide range of secular activities. The religious enthusiasm it tapped has been basic to many movements, but Puritanism was uniquely able to maintain that enthusiasm and to institutionalize it. Rooted in a heightened sense of the individual's confrontation with his God, Puritanism was nonetheless deeply concerned with the idea and the actuality of community. Ostensibly aimed at the past, at the reassertion of ancient values, ironically it contributed greatly to the breakdown of established social patterns.

The emotional heart of Puritanism was its vision of the absolute sovereignty of God and the weakness and worthlessness of man. Most cultures function much of the time to obscure the perception of the frightening discontinuity between the divine and the mortal, but occasionally this vision of the human condition breaks through. At such times man feels profoundly inadequate and strives to find some way of coming to terms with the ground of his own being. Usually such existential breakthroughs soon burn themselves out. While they last man is aflame with a great energizing fire, but such moments quickly pass, for he cannot live with a face-to-face confrontation with God for any great length of time. A major part of the unusual power of Puritanism lay in the fact that it was able to sustain this confrontation for several generations.

As a form of Christianity, as a movement within a great Christian revival, the existential confrontation contained within Puritanism was based on a Christian tradition. The Puritans drew on a religious mood which has been called the Augustinian strain of piety. An emphasis on God as power, on human depravity, and on man's dependency on God for everything, even his own virtues, was the essential root of Puritanism and the most profound source of its energies.

But this Augustinian piety was only one side of Puritan religion. Without an intellectual and institutional structure the piety would have quickly consumed itself. The covenant or federal theology provided that structure. The God whom man had no hope of understanding or of pleasing by his own efforts had voluntarily undertaken to form an agreement by which He would bind Himself to act in ways comprehensible to man. This was no contradiction of His fundamentally unmatchable sovereignty; rather, the voluntary limitation of His power was seen as the highest expression of power and mercy.

This covenant of grace was as vital to Puritan development as the piety. It provided a means by which man could stand to live with the Augustinian vision of God. It was a kind of intellectual container for the emotional heart of the religion. The Puritan typically oscillated in mood between the sense of his worthlessness and powerlessness engendered by the piety and the confidence inspired by the idea of covenant. It was the covenant that differentiated Puritanism from most other evangelical movements which tend to weaken as man grows weary of confronting an angry God. As long as the vision of God and the idea of the covenant remained in vital tension with each other Puritanism remained forcefully alive. When they became disjointed the movement was essentially over.

The concept of the covenant played a number of roles in Puritan life and thought. In addition to the covenant of grace, it provided a part of the rationale for their civil government. Also, the members of a Congregationalist church were united by a covenant. Most important of all in the impact of Puritanism

on later American history was the way in which the early New
Englanders conceived of their special commission from God as a
covenant that gave a peculiar significance to every event in the
community.

Some of the tensions within Puritanism involved more manifestly contradictory tendencies than did that between the piety
and the covenant.

An individual's confrontation with God was an inward and
highly personal event, but it had outward and social consequences. God demanded that the believer manifest his faith
visibly and effectively in the world. Part of the Puritan's duty
was the general reformation of worship and life, and if necessary
all the coercive power of the state could be used to achieve that
end. The church and society must be made to conform to divine
requirements, and individual wills must be bent to the divine
intention.

Yet, as heirs of the Reformation, Puritans respected the individual conscience. They placed great emphasis on the inward,
personal nature of religious experience. Liberty as well as reformation was a part of their program, although it was liberty
only in a very special sense. There was a problem here, one that
was more serious for Congregationalists than for other Puritans.
If the ultimate appeal on earth was to the individual conscience,
how could a uniformity of reformation be imposed? If every
congregation was to be self-governing, what was to prevent the
development of different visions of the truth, of different ref-
ormations? In theory the Puritans had an answer. The Bible,
if properly read by visible saints with the aid of divine guidance
and an educated clergy, would lead in only one direction. When
Congregational churches actually were established in New
England, it became apparent that uniformity could not be
achieved through the careful reading of the Scriptures and the
independence of the congregations was compromised in order to
ensure it. During the Civil War, when the same problem appeared in England under different conditions, it was dealt with
by moderating the demand for uniformity in the acceptance of
a degree of religious toleration. One of the sources of the differ-
entiation of American culture from English is to be found in the

different resolutions of the tension between liberty and reformation in Old and New England.

The Puritan demand that man live actively in this world had other unintended consequences. The belief that economic as well as political activity was sanctified had enormously energizing effects. It may have been that an inhibition on the full application of human efforts to secular tasks was removed as actions in this world came to be seen as congruent with and not opposed to the divine will. Energies released in this way contributed to profound changes throughout Western society.

The conscious Puritan social ideal was organic and static. Puritans believed in a hierarchical order in which there was a place for every man and in which every man knew his place. This would mirror the hierarchical order of God's creation and provide the opportunity for man to exercise virtues appropriate to his station. In demanding that he actively reform society in accordance with this model, Puritanism unleashed forces it could not control. Political activity was sanctified for a large body of believers, and modern habits of political participation were engendered. In the long run this led in a direction quite opposed to the static order that Puritans sought.

Puritan social ideas were also clearly opposed modern capitalism. Some of the conditions they most vehemently opposed could be regarded as symptoms of the beginnings of capitalism. To be sure, the Puritans respected private property, but its use was held to be a concern of the community. Every man was called by God to follow a particular occupation. It was incumbent on him to pursue his calling assiduously as a duty to himself, to his community, and to God. The overt function of the doctrine of the calling was to support the hierarchical conception of society, but the actual consequences of the energetic pursuit of a calling could be quite different. How was a merchant to follow his calling as effectively as he could and at the same time not move out of his proper place in society? The difficulty is compounded when it is realized that Puritans applied the doctrine of the calling to income as well as work. Investment was preferred to consumption, since it was of greater service to the community and to God.

The Puritans as Puritans had no desire to further the development of capitalism, yet the energies released by the sanctification of work contributed greatly to the increased productivity of modern economic life. Puritan merchants in dutifully pursuing their calling contributed to the growth of a market-regulated economy and modern economic individualism. Here Puritan intentions clearly had ironic consequences.

The American Puritans were involved in yet another basic contradiction. They had been called by God to remove themselves into the wilderness not for their material betterment nor even for their own spiritual welfare but as agents of universal reformation. The independence of their churches did not imply any rejection of the idea of catholicism. They were acting for all mankind, and when history caught up with Massachusetts they would be vindicated. They were a special people, a chosen nation, but they were chosen as representatives of the world. Yet their sense of mission, of chosenness, could engender an arrogance contradictory to their ideal of universality. When English history moved in a direction that indicated that the world was not going to follow the New England way, it became increasingly hard to balance the sense of universality against the idea of being chosen, to withstand the feeling that they had a mission against the rest of mankind rather than for it.

In examining the significance of Puritanism, we must be aware of the tensions in our own relationship to it. As modern Americans we are a part of a culture that Puritanism helped to shape. It is altogether proper for us to seek in it some of the sources of modernism and Americanism if we remember always that the Puritans intended to be neither modern nor American. They sought only to worship God and to create a community that would sustain that worship. The art of historical understanding requires that we maintain a balance between the questions we would ask of the past and the recognition that men of the past saw their world very differently from the way we see it.

The following selections have been chosen as illustrations of, and comments on, the tensions of early American Puritanism. In the seventeenth century materials I have modernized spelling and punctuation only as far as needed for easy comprehension. Throughout I have eliminated all footnotes except those essential to the understanding of the text.

Richard Reinitz

Geneva, New York

PART ONE

Piety and Intellect

1

Perry Miller
The Piety and the Federal Theology

Perry Miller was the greatest of all historians of American Puritanism. In a number of books and articles published between the 1930's and the 1960's he explored the depths of Puritan thought and feeling. The corpus of Miller's work on Puritanism constitutes the most complete picture we have of any such complex movement in all American history. Although in some particulars it has been modified by subsequent research, that picture is still the starting point for anyone who would understand the American Puritans.

The New England Mind: The Seventeenth Century lays out a complex and detailed map of fundamental Puritan ideas in all their intricate correlations. In the following selections Miller describes the intense religious feeling at the center of Puritanism and the theological construct which made it possible for men to live with that feeling.

SOURCE. Reprinted by permission of the publisher from Perry Miller, *The New England Mind: The Seventeenth Century*, pp. 4–9, 375–385. Cambridge, Mass.: Harvard University Press. Copyright 1939 by Perry Miller; 1954 by the President and Fellows of Harvard College.

THE AUGUSTINIAN STRAIN OF PIETY

When the wave of religious assertion which we call Puritanism is considered in the broad perspective of Christian history, it appears no longer as a unique phenomenon, peculiar to England of the seventeenth century, but as one more instance of a recurrent spiritual answer to interrogations eternally posed by human existence. The peculiar accidents of time and place did indeed entice Puritanism into entertaining a variety of ideas which were the features of its epoch, yet it was animated by a spirit that was not peculiar to the seventeenth century or to East Anglia and New England. The major part of this volume will necessarily be occupied with local and temporal characteristics, but these were not the substance or the soul of the movement. As Puritanism developed it became more and more encased in technical jargon and increasingly distracted by economic and social issues; as it waned it partook more of the qualities of one age and became less of a gospel for all time. But as long as it remained alive, its real being was not in its doctrines but behind them; the impetus came from an urgent sense of man's predicament, from a mood so deep that it could never be completely articulated. Inside the shell of its theology and beneath the surface coloring of its political theory, Puritanism was yet another manifestation of a piety to which some men are probably always inclined and which in certain conjunctions appeals irresistibly to large numbers of exceptionally vigorous spirits.

I venture to call this piety Augustinian, not because it depended directly upon Augustine—though one might demonstrate that he exerted the greatest single influence upon Puritan thought next to that of the Bible itself, and in reality a greater one than did John Calvin—nor because Puritan thought and Augustine's harmonize in every particular. Some aspects of his work, his defense of the authority of the church and of the magical efficacy of the sacraments, were ignored by Puritans as by other Protestants. I call it Augustinian simply because Augustine is the arch-exemplar of a religious frame of mind of which Puritanism is only one instance out of many in fifteen hundred years of religious history. For a number of reasons many persons in late sixteenth-century England found themselves looking upon the problems of life very nearly as Augustine had viewed them, and, for reasons still difficult to expound, the number of such persons increased during the next six or seven decades. In the 1630's some twenty thousand of them, avowedly inspired by their religious views, settled New England and thus served to leave the impress of Augustine upon the American character. In England, as these spirits became more numerous, they came into conflict with other Englishmen, some of whom were certainly no less pious and no less Christian, but in very different fashions. When Puritans debated with Richard Hooker, the apologist of the Anglican church, they spoke at cross-purposes, for his intellectual affinites were entirely with Thomas Aquinas and scholastic tradition. The Puritans also were scholastics, but though they and Richard Hooker might use the same terms, their emphases were irreconcilable, and as between the two there can be no doubt that in the writings of Hooker's enemies we shall find the turn of mind and sense of values, even sometimes the very accent, of Augustine. There survive hundreds of Puritan diaries and thousands of Puritan sermons, but we can read the inward meaning of them all in the *Confessions.*

Puritan theology was an effort to externalize and systematize this subjective mood. Piety was the inspiration for Puritan heroism and the impetus in the charge of Puritan Ironsides; it also made sharp the edge of Puritan cruelty and justified the Puritan in his persecution of disagreement. It inspired Puritan idealism and encouraged Puritan snobbery. It was something that men either had or had not, it could not be taught or acquired. It was foolishness and fanaticism to their opponents, but to themselves it was life eternal. Surely most of the first settlers of New England had it; in later generations most of those who did not have it pretended to it. It blazed most clearly and most fiercely in the person of Jonathan Edwards, but Emerson was illuminated, though from afar, by its rays, and it smoldered in the recesses of Hawthorne's intuitions. It cannot be portrayed by description; to be presented adequately there is need for a Puritan who is also a dramatic artist, and Bunyan alone fulfills the two requirements. But in order that we may pursue the story of expression in New England, that we may find larger meanings in the formal intellectual developments, it has seemed advisable to attempt a description of this piety. The subsequent narrative will, I hope, take on added significance as an episode in the history of humanity if we can first of all conceive, even though we do not share, the living reality of the spirit that motivated this particular group of men. Thus I am here endeavoring to portray the piety rather than the abstract theology in which it was embodied, to present it not in the dry metaphysics of scholastic divines, but in such plain statements, thrown deliberately into the present tense, as the most scholastic of the clergy could utter, fortunately, in their less controversial moods. I shall undoubtedly do the material a certain violence by speaking of the sharply defined concepts of systematic divinity in the looser and vaguer language of human passion; yet the great structure of the Puritan creed, ostensibly erected upon the foundation of logic, will have meaning to most students today only when they perceive that it rested upon a deep-lying conviction that the universe conformed to a definite, ascertainable truth, and that human existence was to be had only upon the terms imposed by this truth.

Such a chapter as I am now attempting could never have been written by any true Puritan, for I am seeking to delineate the inner core of Puritan sensibility apart from the dialectic and the doctrine. In Puritan life the two were never so separated; they were indeed inseparable, for systematic theology, now become wearisome to the majority of men, provided Puritans with completely satisfying symbols; it dramatized the needs of the soul exactly as does some great poem or work of art. The religious emotion could not have existed, for them at least, except within the framework of dogma. Although we, starting from other assumptions and thinking as historians rather than as Puritans, may now ask what underlay the doctrine of predestination before we undertake to trace its evolution through the next two centuries, for Puritans themselves such a dissociation of the meaning from the formula was inconceivable. They saw no opposition between the spirit of religion and the letter of theology, between faith and its intellectualization, and they would have found no sense whatsoever in modern contentions that the words and parables of Christ may be understood without reference to an organized body of abstractions. It should also be

confessed at once that many of the statements made in this chapter will be found at variance with the later sections. This is not
to be wondered at when the nature of theology, and more particularly of theologians, is considered. Puritan sensibility was
truly unified and coherent; but it was articulated only in dogmas
and logical deductions. Dogmas can easily become severed from
their emotional background, even by those who believe in them
most passionately, where upon they often become counters in an
intricate intellectual chess games and lose all semblance of their
original meaning. The effort to trace these permutations is
triply difficult because transformation may come through a
subtle shift in emotional connotation, or the same connotation
may be preserved within a gradual reformulation of the doctrine,
or else there may be a step-by-step progression in both signification and doctrine. It is not surprising, therefore, that among
the basic assurances of early seventeenth-century Puritanism,
after the Protestant cause had already been argued for a century,
there should have been some that did not wholly correspond to
the verbal symbols. Finally, we must remember that religion was
not the sole, though it was indeed the predominant interest of
the Puritans. They were skilled in many sciences besides theology, and they inevitably drew ideas from these sources, sometimes deliberately, more often unwittingly. We shall find that
such ideas existed in their minds in more or less happy fusion
with their religious convictions, and that when there was latent
opposition among them the Puritans themselves were at best only
dimly aware of it. These considerations are almost too elementary to need restatement; still, they indicate cautions to be
observed as we seek for a definition of Puritan piety, of the
temperamental bias behind the thought, before we undertake to
examine the thought itself.

It would, however, be a grave mistake to regard Puritan piety
solely as an affair of temperament. We may declare that Puritans
universalized their own neurasthenia; they themselves believed
that their fears and anxieties came from clear-eyed perception of
things as they are. We may say that they derived their ideas
from the Bible, from Augustine and Calvin, Petrus Ramus and
William Perkins, and that they were influenced by such and such

factors in the environment. They believed that, the facts being
what they are, one deduction alone was possible. The facts were
in the Bible, which was of course the Word of God, but they were
also in experience, and a man did not need the sermons of a
godly minister to perceive the terms upon which all men struggle
through existence; he needed merely to look about him. "Look,"
says the Puritan preacher, the doctrine is "as in nature, reason
teacheth and experience evidenceth"; to deny it "is to go against
the experience of all ages, the common sense of all men." It is
obvious that man dwells in a splendid universe, a magnificent
expanse of earth and sky and heavens, which manifestly is built
upon a majestic plan, maintains some mightly design, though
man himself cannot grasp it. Yet for him it is not a pleasant or
satisfying world. In his few moments of respite from labor or
from his enemies, he dreams that this very universe might indeed
be perfect, its laws operating just as now they seem to do, and yet
he and it somehow be in full accord. The very ease with which
he can frame this image to himself makes reality all the more
mocking; the world does give men food and drink, but it gives
grudgingly, and when "the world says, peace, peace, then suddenly destruction comes upon them as a whirlwind." It is only
too clear that man is not at home within this universe, and yet
that he is not good enough to deserve a better; he is out of touch
with the grand harmony, he is an incongruous being amid the
creatures, a blemish and a blot upon the face of nature. There
is the majestical roof, fretted with golden fire, and likewise there
is man, a noble work that delights not himself. It is certain that
the works of God "were all Good and Beautiful as they came
out of his Hands," but equally certain that some deed of man
"has put all out of Order, and has brought Confusion and Desolation on the works of God." There are moments of vision when
the living spirit seems to circulate in his veins, when man is in
accord with the totality of things, when his life ceases to be a
burden to him and separateness is ecstatically overcome by
mysterious participation in the whole. In such moments he has
intimations of rightness, of a state of being in which he and his
environment achieve perfect harmony, just as in his imagination
he has fancied that once he did dwell in paradise. When these

moments have passed he endeavors to live by their fading light, struggling against imperfection in the memory of their perfection, or else he falls back, wearied and rebellious, into cynicism and acrimony. All about him he sees men without this illumination, exemplifying the horrors of their detached and forlorn condition. They murder, malign, and betray each other, they are not to be relied upon, they wear themselves out in the chains of lust, their lives have no meaning, their virtues are pretenses and their vices unprofitable. What wonder that we see exorbitancies and confusions in human societies, "when fools and madmen have gotten the reins in their necks, and act all their own pleasure without any control"? Mortals pursue illusions, and success inspires only disgust or despair. They seek forgetfulness in idolatries and narcotics, or delude themselves in sophistical reasonings, and they die at last cursing the day they were born or clutching at the clay feet of their superstitions. Puritans did not believe that they saw things in these terms merely because they were victims of melancholia, but because such things were there to be seen. The so-called "Five Points" of Calvinism were simply a scholastical fashion of saying this much, and to living Calvinists they did not signify five abstract dicta, but a description of the plight of humanity.

The ultimate reason of all things they called God, the dream of a possible harmony between man and his environment they named Eden, the actual fact of disharmony they denominated sin, the moment of illumination was to them divine grace, the effort to live in the strength of that illumination was faith, and the failure to abide by it was reprobation. The heart of this piety was its sense of the overwhelming anguish to which man is always subject, and its appeal to anguish-torn humanity has always been its promise of comfort and of ultimate triumph. The Augustinian strain of piety flows from man's desire to transcend his imperfect self, to open channels for the influx of an energy which pervades the world, but with which he himself is inadequately supplied. It takes flight from the realization that the natural man, standing alone in the universe, is not only minute and insignificant, but completely out of touch with both justice and beauty. It cries out for forgiveness of the sins by which he has cut himself off from full and joyous participation. It proceeds upon the indomitable conviction that man, a part of created being, must once have been happy, though now he is everywhere miserable. It draws sustenance from the moments of exaltation in which glimpses of the original happiness are attained, a bliss which, though seen but faintly, extinguishes by contrast all other delights. It finds the infinite variety of the world's misery reducible to a concrete problem, the relation of the individual to the One. The substance of Augustine's message is this: "Deum et animam scire cupio. Nihilne plus? Nihil omnino." If man once achieved knowledge of God and of his soul, the answer to all other questions would soon follow. The irrepressible demand of the soul for this knowledge is the driving force of the piety. On the one hand, the facts are those ordained by a just God; on the other hand, there are the desires of the soul. The soul must be satisfied, but the facts cannot be denied. There can be no separating the attainment of happiness from the attainment of truth. Solutions which pass lightly over the unpleasant or ignore intractable realities are doomed to failure; so also are those in which the aspirations of the spirit are given insubstantial answers. Wherever the spokesmen for this strain of piety appear, whether in fifth-century Rome or seventeenth-century New England, this is the burden of their sermon, the substance of assertion and the problem for resolution. To the extent that the Puritan generations in New England were able to think and to express their thought, this was the inevitable preoccupation of their discourse.

Long before the seventeenth century theologians had discovered that the endeavor to formulate this piety centered upon certain fundamental conceptions: God, sin, and regeneration. Each of these ideas received elaborate exposition in the creeds, confessions, and institutes that streamed from the inexhaustible inkwells of Protestant writers; each of them was divided into subdoctrines, which in turn were sorted into still further theological ramifications. Meanwhile, the basic ideas in their essential meanings remained simple and inviolate. "God" was a word to stand for the majesty and perfection which gleam through the fabric of the world; He was Being, hardly apprehensible to man, yet whose existence man must posit, not so much as *a* being but as *The* Being, the beginning of things and the sustainer, the principle of universal harmony and the guide. "Sin" was in effect a way of setting forth disharmony, of describing man's inability to live decently, his cruelties and his crimes, and also a way of accounting for the accidents, the diseases, and the sorrows which every day befall the good and the bad. On the definition of "regeneration" Protestants expended their greatest ingenuity and differed among themselves most furiously, exemplifying in their controversies all the vindictiveness which they deplored in other men as an evidence of innate depravity. Yet to all Protestants the general conception was the same; it meant substantially that there existed a way in which supernal beauty could be carried across the gulf of separation. It was an inward experience in which the disorder of the universe was righted, when at least some men were brought into harmony with the divine plan. It was the solution to the double problem of religion, reconciling the soul to fact and yet satisfying its desires. It joined God and man, the whole and the particle. God reached out to man with His grace, man reached out to God with his faith. Regeneration meant the repose and the happiness toward which all men grope, because God "is the most pure, perfect, universall, primary, unchangeable, communicative, desirable, and delightfull good: the efficient, patterne, and utmost end *of all good;* without whom there is neither naturall, morall, nor spirituall good in any creature." All men seek the good, but only those who in unforgettable moments are ravished by it ever come to know it.

. . . .

THE COVENANT OF GRACE

The substance of the federal theory can be stated briefly, though its implications could be investigated indefinitely. By the word "covenant" federal theologians understood just such a contract as was used among men of business, a bond or a mortgage, an agreement between two parties, signed and sworn to, and binding upon both. It was usually defined as "A mutual agreement between parties upon Articles or Propositions on both side, so that each party is tied and bound to performe his own conditions." In his *Cases of Conscience,* Ames described the ordinary contract, emphasizing that its essence was voluntary engagement. It was, he said, a free consent, a treaty arrived at by the participants without constraint, each of whom honestly intends to live up to the terms and who, to record his willingness and his obligations, expresses them by an outward sign, by a document attested and sealed. Because each enters the pact of his own volition, each has a right to expect from the other a fulfillment to the letter; "the forme doth require internall, and essentiall the upright dealing of the Contractor, to bee true, and sincere." Always the fundamental point, insisted upon *ad nauseam,* was the voluntaristic basis of the undertaking: "Where two Parties do stand mutually obliged one to another in voluntary Agreement, there is a Covenant." None ever need exist unless both signatories wish it; before it, they are free as the air, but once having set their hands to it, they are no longer at liberty, they are irrevocably shackled. "Natural Necessity destroys the very nature of a Covenant," said Willard, for it must be "a voluntary obligation between persons about things wherein they enjoy a freedom of Will, and have a power to choose or refuse," it must be "a deliberate thing wherein there is a Counsel and a Consent between Rational and free Agents." Because a man takes a covenant upon himself, it is the strongest tie by which he can ever be bound. In a covenant he is infinitely more liable than in a promise, more obligated than by a law, more involved than in a testament, more answerable than for his oath. An oath may attest a mistake, but a covenant guarantees truth. A promise calls for some future good, a law for some performance, but a covenant calls for both. A law depends upon the sovereignty of the law-giver, who is able to save or destroy and is under no compulsion to do the one rather than the other; a testament is grounded on the will of the testator, who gives without the consent of his beneficiaries; but a covenant "differs from them both, in this, that it requires the consent and agreement of both parties, and therein each party binds himself freely to the performance of several conditions each to other." An absolute monarch can change his laws every day, forswear his oaths, make promises and break them by the score, rewrite his testament as often as he pleases, but once he enters a covenant, though with but the humblest of his peasants, he is held as with hoops of steel. One who owes a debt of money may abscond, or of friendship may prove false, the day laborer may go elsewhere tomorrow; but when a man has made a covenant with his landlord, his friend, or his employer, he can never escape his commitment. Starting from absolute independence, the covenant leads to mutual subjection; in a universe where nothing seems certain, it alone produces certainty; in a society where men cannot be relied upon, it creates reliability. It is the only point at which might and weakness can meet on a footing of right.

The federal theology appropriated this concept and fastened it upon both God and man. "We must not make Gods Covenant with man, so far to differ from Covenants between man and man, as to make it no Covenant at all." It found in the idea a key to the history of the universe, the innermost meaning of divine revelation, the foundation of law in the apparent lawlessness of nature. It held that man, viewed simply as part of creation, is the serf of his lord, the subject of his prince, but that viewed as the rational part of that creation, he stands also in relation to God as one man in covenant with another. He who creates is under no obligation to those whom he creates; God might slay His creatures, or torture them, or forget them, and none could call Him to account, but in the Covenant He has voluntarily tied His hands, willingly agreed to a set of terms. There have been "as it were indentures drawne betweene God and man, conditions on both sides agreed upon," and in place of an ontological relation, a connection determined by brute necessity and the ineluctable order of things, is substituted an equally certain but more honorable relation of assent. God forgoes what is His by right divine, preferring a spontaneous to an enforced service. His gesture is pure graciousness. Covenants between men concern things "which either were not due before, or were not thought to be due, which are made firme, stable and due by the very Covenant, so that by the Covenant new right is acquired or caused, either to one or both, who Covenant betwixt themselves of any matter." Out of His mere pleasure, God in the Covenant gives men something new, something over and above their mere existence, something gratuitous, and then by affixing his seal to the grant translates the bestowed privilege into a right. He who might rule by fiat limits Himself to a contract; He who could exact tribute to the last farthing consents to parliamentary taxation. The covenant between God and man is an agreement of unequals upon just and equal terms, "in which God promises true happinesse to man, and man engages himself by promise for performance of what God requires." It may be, as Preston said, a difficult point to grasp, "yet you must know it, for it is the ground of all you hope for, it is that that euery man is built vpon, you haue no other ground but this, God hath made a Couenant with you, and you are in Couenant with him."

According to the federalists, God has never dealt with mankind except in this way. "As soon as God had Created man, he plighted a Covenant with him." He proposed that if Adam would perform certain things, Adam and his posterity should be rewarded with eternal life, and He laid down the specific conditions in the moral law, which He implanted in Adam's heart. Hence the terms of this first covenant, the Covenant of Works, are what we know as the law of nature, and by failing to keep them, Adam, and we as his posterity, incurred the just penalty. But God did not rest there. Beginning with Abraham, He commenced a new covenant, the Covenant of Grace, which is a true contract of mutual obligation, but this time the condition for the mortal partner is not a deed but a faith: "sayth the *Lord*, this is the Covenant that I wil make on my part, *I will be thy God* . . . you shall haue all things in me that your hearts can desire: The *Covenant* againe, that I require on your part, is, that you be *perfect with me*," but the perfection required is in the heart rather than in the hands, "so that though a man be subject to infirmities yet, if he haue a single heart, an vpright heart, the *Lord* accepts it." Because fallen man is unable any longer to fulfill the moral law, God in the person of Christ takes the task upon Himself; the Covenant of Works is not recalled but kept by God in the place of man, while in the new Covenant those who will believe in the Redeemer have His righteousness ascribed to them and so are "justified" according to the new terms. Recognizing the now bankrupt condition of the tenant, the landlord guarantees in a new lease to provide him the wherewithal to pay his rent and

keep a roof over his head, provided he will believe in the land-
lord's goodness and show what gratitude he can. "In the Covenant of workes, a man is left to himselfe, to stand by his own
strength; But in the Covenant of grace, God undertakes for us,
to keep us through faith." We have only to pledge that, when it
is given us, we will avail ourselves of the assistance which makes
faith possible, and Sibbes therefore defined the Covenant of
Grace in terms common to all the writers:

"It has pleased the great God to enter into a treaty and covenant of agreement with us his poor creatures, the articles of
which agreement are here comprised. God, for his part, undertakes to convey all that concerns our happiness, upon our receiving of them, by believing on him. Every one in particular that
recites these articles from a spirit of faith makes good this
condition."

If a man can believe, he has done his part; God then must needs
redeem him and glorify him.

The new Covenant was first propounded, according to these
theologians, to Abraham; the seventeenth chapter of Genesis was
their key text, upon which most of their works were a com-
mentary, and Deuteronomy they called "The Book of the Covenant." The condition for Abraham was faith, exactly as for us,
though he was required to believe that Christ would come; since
the resurrection, we have merely to belive that He has come and
that He is "surety" for the new Covenant. But from Abraham
to the settlers of New England, there is one and the same bond
between God and man. "We are the children of *Abraham;* and
therefore we are under *Abrahams* covenant." Abraham, according to Joshua Moody, "was the *Great Pattern Believer,*" and
Cobbett spoke of the Covenant of Grace as "the old Charter of
Abrahams covenant." The transaction upon the plain of Mamre
in Hebron was not a mere promise on God's part, it was a complete commitment, for to these authors the idea that God merely
promised was not enough. "It is impertinent to put a difference
betweene the promise and the Covenant ... The promise of God
and his Covenant ... are ordinarily put one for another." The
Covenant, its origin, its progressive unfolding, its culmination,
was thus the meaning of history, that which made intelligible the

whole story of mankind. It was "the very Basis on which all that follows is built, and unto which it must be referred"; God never does anything for His people unless "he doth it by vertue of, and according to his Covenant," and the number of the saints is accomplished, not merely through the means, but through the means as agents of the Covenant:

"God conveys his salvation by way of covenant, and he doth it to those onely that are in covenant with him . . . This covenant must every soule enter into, every particular soul must enter into a particular covenant with God; out of this way there is no life."

So Puritan divines of the seventeenth century, perceiving the amplitude of this doctrine, broke like Cotton into hymns of delight: "This is such an Argument as the strength and wisdome of men and Angels cannot unfold," and then, like good Puritans and good Ramists, set themselves to unfolding it " (as the Lord hath revealed it) I mean, plainly and familiarly."

It may seem at first sight that some over-ingenious lawyer and no man of deep piety constructed this legalized version of Biblical history, and we may pardonably wonder how much it really clarified the murk of Calvinism. But Puritan divines had not studied dialectic for nothing; give them this broad premise, backed with copious Scriptural warrants, and they were ready to deduce from it the most gratifying conclusions, for it offered what no other single doctrine could provide, a scheme including both God and man within a single frame, a point at which, without doing violence to their respective natures, both could meet and converse. The Covenant was a gift of God, yet it entailed responsibility on Him as well as upon men. If the orthodox could answer Arminians and Antinomians only when they had set forth the character of God with greater precision, and if they could lay to rest doubts about moral obedience and personal assurance only when they had shown how each was compatible with the facts of human depravity and irresistible grace, then the covenant theory responded perfectly to their necessities. As for the nature of God, the concept of voluntary limitation did away with all difficulties, and as for morality and assurance, the con-

cept of a covenant with conditions answered the objections of all
heretics.

The God of the Covenant was still the ancient Puritan
Jehovah, still a hidden and inexpressible essence, still an im-
penetrable "secresie", but the covenant theology seized avidly
upon the distinction, always so precious to Augustinian thinking,
between His secret and His revealed will. Arminius mistook His
enacted moral statutes for His innermost being, and Antinomians
confused His emanation with Himself; both forgot that He has
first an "absolute" and then an "Ordinate Power," that the
second is not so much different from the first, "but the former
considered, as God hath pleased to set limits or bounds to it by
the Decree." He has an "essential" justice, which is in Him
necessarily and by which He can do no wrong, but also a
"relative" justice, "which is in him freely, that is, it hath no
necessary connexion with the Being of God," and from which
"flows his proceeding with men according to the Law of righteousness freely constituted between him and them." The heretics
forgot that while He rules the cosmos by His absolute power and
His essential justice, He promulgates commandments or bestows
grace by a special extension of Himself over and above the
ordinary, by a power of specific ordination and a justice relative
to circumstances. By the concept of a voluntary contract the theologians sundered the outward manifestation from the inner
principle, and confined it in an irrevocable bond, so that the
finite could thereafter treat with the infinite. They achieved this
remarkable feat without dethroning His omnipotence, without
circumscribing His sovereignty, by the plausible device of at-
tributing the instigation of the deal to Him. He alone, of His
own unfettered will, proposed that He be chained. "It's Gods
usual way so to deal, not that he is tyed, or hath tied himself to
this manner of dealing upon necessity, but that he hath expressed
it to be his good pleasure so to dispense himself." In Himself He
remains an unknowable transcendence but in His Covenant He
freely takes upon Himself a local habitation and a name; outside
the pale He is wholly irresponsible, but within it He has placed

Himself under a yoke. In His nature He remains above all law, outside all morality, beyond all reason, but in the Covenant He is ruled by a law, constrained to be moral, committed to sweet reasonableness. God as the source of all being, not only of things that are, but of all those things that might be, the boundless realm of possibility, was the starting point of piety, of physics, and of technologia, but simple piety had nothing more to build upon than the particular articles He had arbitrarily revealed, physics could merely report the order it had pleased Him to create, technologia could arrange in the arts just such actualities as He had despotically selected out of the unnumbered potentials, whereas the federal theology founded its doctrine upon the immovable basis of a sealed covenant, upon a just agreement eternally sanctioned, from which the supreme power of the universe could never depart by a hair's breadth. Dialectic invented whatever arguments were embodied in things and arranged them in imitation of factual dispositions; it was fortunately able to describe a rational universe, but the rationality was wholly fortuitous. As far as logic itself could tell, the logic of the universe was a happy incident in God's decree, and at any moment, by a flicker of His hand, He might send it sprawling into chaos. But in His Covenant the kaleidoscopic world came to rest. God gives some amount of certainty by His Word, and "not onely his bare Word, but a binding Word, his promises," but the ultimate certitude is not "onely Promises, but his Covenant, founded upon a full satisfaction made to his justice." Within the Covenant, as "in all other royall patents, and grants of princely grace, and bounty," permanence reigns. Within this circuit, infinitesimal as compared with His essence, but spacious enough to include all humanity, two and two will always equal four, a cause will have its effect, and the fulfillment of conditions never fail of the assured reward. Within this circumference, God speaks no longer with unpredictable fury, but in words of comfort:

"I will not onely tell thee what I am able to doe, I will not onely expresse to thee in generall, that I will deale well with thee, that I haue a willingnesse and ability to recompence thee, if thou walke before mee, and serue mee, and bee perfect; but I

am willing to enter into Couenant with thee, that is, I will binde
my selfe, I will ingage my selfe, I will enter into bond, as it were,
I will not bee at liberty any more, but I am willing euen to make
a Couenant, a compact and agreement with thee."

Thus we may cease being apprehensive over His hidden terrors
and may assume that in our experience He will abide by definite
regulations. He will no longer do all the unimaginable things
He can do, but "all things which he hath promised to doe." As
John Cotton said, professing all reverence, God has "muffled"
Himself as with a cloak, "He cannot strike as he would . . . he is
so compassed about with his nature and property, and Covenant,
that he hath no liberty to strike." Hooker joined the chorus:
"We have the Lord in bonds, for the fulfilling his part of the
Covenant: He hath taken a corporall Oath of it, that He will do
it." Because the Covenant of Grace, said Willard, "ariseth from,
or is grounded upon the occasions of dealing or trading between
one and another," it too demands perfect sincerity of the con-
tractors, and "each Party may be secured from suffereing any
damage by the other; but may be able to claim and recover the
performance." Having created the universe, the creator takes
His place within it upon the same level with His creatures,
becoming morally responsible and liable, should He ever take
unfair advantage of His might, to be arrested, prosecuted, and
fined.

Meanwhile, the balance of His attributes was impeccably preserved. His sovereignty was not infringed, for He entered the
Covenant under no other pressure than His free assent. He was
still the absolute monarch, although He had given His subjects
a bill of inviolable rights. He remained thoroughly just, exacting
the full penalty for transgressions of the first Covenant, and yet
showed Himself in the second Covenant extravagantly merciful.
"It is not in our reach to understand how ever this could have
been done declaratively . . . but in the way of a Covenant." In
fact, it almost seems as though Puritan theologians, having dwelt
for years upon the implacable rigor of divine justice and being
forced, in spite of the balance, to present sovereignty as the
dominant attribute, were intensely relieved to come upon the

covenant doctrine as at last something tangible to adduce in pleading that God was also gracious. . . .

For Puritans the instruction provided by the Covenant of Grace upon the nature of God was merely preliminary to its instructions concerning salvation and ethics. The essential point was that it made possible a voluntary relation of man to God, even though man's will was considered impotent and God's grace irresistible. He who by His absolute dominion might "have dealt with Men in a way of Soveraignty only, requiring Duty and Obedience from them, without any promise of reward," nevertheless "has seen Good to transact with them in a Covenant way." He now occupies, not the throne of a tyrant, but the seat "of a righteous Judge, and cannot dispense with his own Law, because his Truth and Righteousness engage him to it." Therefore He fixes upon this scheme that there should be on the side of man a voluntary return, a sincere pledge that will have some elements of spontaneity. He made both the Covenants "conditional," that of Grace no less than that of Works, so that they would be relations founded upon mutual stipulations, not upon brute fact. He forewent his "unconfined prerogative" and "voluntarily obliged himself in the threatning annexed to his own Command"; does it not follow, then, that there is a double engagement, "by the one we are bound to God, and by the other God is bound to us"? As creator He is absolute, "but yet that man might not think much to yield obedience, God is pleas'd to engage himself to a recompense." The all-important fact for the Puritan parson, as each Sabbath he ascended his pulpit steps, was that he could promise the recompense to an active and generous obedience.

Even so, the good parson had his work cut out for him. His congregation knew, if they knew nothing else, that salvation by faith and not by works was orthodoxy, and that any hedging of this point was heresy. He had to explain to them that when faith was viewed not as a simple act of belief, but as the condition of a covenant, it became in itself, as it were, a "work," involving in the inward act an obligation to external behavior. He explained the connection a thousand times over, so insistently that we may suspect he was none too confident of his own logic. He put this construction upon faith by commencing always with the distinction between God's natural rule and God's special dispensation. In the natural rule, where God does everything "absolutely and simply without any condition, as the creation and regiment of the world," He acts as in the pestilence and the hurricane. Were men regenerated under this rule they would fall as ripe fruit to the ground or be driven as dead leaves before the wind. But when God acts by his "signifying" will, He "willeth some things for some other thing, with condition, and so we say, because that the condition annexed is a signe of the will, that God doth so will." He is equally sovereign in either manifestation, but whereas in the first He merely says, "Let the hurricane strike," in the other He says, "I will save those that believe." Thus belief, although given by His grace, is not quite the same thing as understood by unlearned piety; it does not merely regenerate man's faculties, but also enables the revived faculties, the reason and will, to believe, and through believing to give free, rational, and voluntary consent to a contract. In other words, sanctification was not expected to follow upon justification automatically, it was not left for God to work while the man stood idly by, but the will was enlisted and pledged, according to the stipulation, to see that all the faculties bestirred themselves. The covenanted saint does not supinely believe, but does the best he can, and God will not hold his failures against him; having pledged himself, the saint has taken the responsibility upon himself and agreed to coöperate with God in the difficult labor. He is not as a child to whom for no reason a fatuous parent gives a shilling, but as one informed by a wise father that he may have a penny if he washes his face and hands and improves his manners. Man does not recline and say, "Let God do it," but reflects, "I am engaged by my own consent, I must try to make good my word." The grace which enables some to try, and without which the others will not attempt anything creditable, is wholly an arbitrary favor dispensed in a way of sovereignty to those whom God has forever predestined to election, yet to the elect it is also dispensed in a way of free compact, so that they treat about it with God upon a voluntary basis. Hence they are covenanted to sainthood, not forced into it, and they are to be

saved for trying, not for succeeding, whereas the reprobate are
eternally damned, not for failing, but for not trying.

In order that men should not presume upon the "Absolute
Promises" of the Covenant to give over trying, the federal God,
who is exceedingly shrewd, perfected the adroit device of in-
corporating the Covenant of Works into the Covenant of Grace,
not as the condition of salvation but as the rule of righteousness.
No man can any longer be saved by fulfilling the law, even
should he be capable of it, for the Covenant of Works is not now
in force between God and man, and God is not bound by it. But
the law, which was the condition of that Covenant, remains "as
the unchangeable rule of life and manners, according to which
persons in Covenant ought to walke before and with the Lord,
and in this sense it belongs to the Covenant of grace." It is no
longer one of the terms of the pact, but it is there as the "school-
master" of the new terms, to teach the goal toward which a believer must incessantly strive, even while knowing that he cannot
encompass it. Man still owes a debt to the law; he who borrows
money "stands bound to the Creditor to answer the Debt, though
his state alter, and he be impoverished, and made unable to pay,
yet his Bond for payment continues in full force against him,
and he will be constrained to make it good." The faculties,
restored by grace to some semblance of their original liberty, are
not kept in ignorance of their duties: "For the Morall Law, the
Law of the ten Commandements, we are dead also to the *covenant*
of that law, though not to the *command* of it." Even before conversion, even while we are still impotent, the law is our school-
master, teaching what we should do, whether we can or not. It
is indeed a rigorous pedagogue; we stand in relation to the law,
said Hooker in one of the commercial metaphors so constantly
employed in all preaching of this doctrine, as a tenant to a land-
lord, to whom the tenant owes rent for many years' occupancy
and to whom, as he is about to be put out, he offers a half-year's
fee:

"Will this man thinke that he hath now satisfied his Land-lord?
if he should say, now Land-lord, I hope you are contented, and
all is answered & I have fully paid all that is betweene you and

mee, you Land-lords would be ready to reply thus, and say, This
satisfies me for the last halfe yeare past, but who payes for the
odde hundreds?"

Realizing that we cannot fulfill the law, that we cannot pay for
the odd hundreds, we flee to Christ for the assistance of grace.
Knowledge of the law is thus for the unregenerate a "means" of
conversion; it sets "home the burden of their sins unto their
souls, thereby to drive them to feel their great need of the Lord."
Once again God is dealing with man as a reasonable creature,
giving him a rule that can be known in the understanding and
embraced in the will. But according to the federal theology,
conversion is synonymous with taking a covenant; we do not
merely flee to Christ from the terrors of the law, but we strike a
bargain with Him, and if we turn to Him in acknowledging our
inability otherwise to pay our debt to the law, then with the help
of His grace we should naturally undertake to fulfill our obligation. That we should use grace to satisfy the law would certainly
be one of the conditions of the Covenant of Grace: "For God
never calleth any unto fellowship with himself in a Covenant of
Grace, but ordinarily he first bringeth them into a Covenant of
Works." God as sovereign may do what He will, but He "doth
not absolutely promise life unto any, he doth not say to any
soule, I will save you and bring you to life, though you continue
impenitent & unbelieving," but He commands us to repent and
believe, "and then promises that in the way of faith and repentance, he will save us." So for us who have faith and have re-
pented, "He prescribes a way of life for us to walk in, that so
wee may obtaine the salvation which he hath promised." Thus
the Covenant of Grace becomes a "conditional" covenant; the
condition is faith, but covenant-faith has in the law a way prescribed for it to walk in, and faith as the fulfillment of a covenant
obliges the believer so to walk, whereas unsophisticated piety
naively supposes that faith in itself is adequate for salvation re-
gardless of how it walks.

2   *Thomas Hooker*
Human Sin and the Disruption of Divine Order

The Puritan began with the realization that sin, which separated him from God, was an integral part of his nature. The deeply felt recognition of his own personal sinfulness was the cause of the greatest anguish to the Puritan but it was, as well, the beginning of hope, for it was only in the emotional knowledge of sin that grace could begin to operate.

Thomas Hooker here presents the emotional heart of Puritanism in terms at once universal and highly personal. Hooker was one of the most distinguished and learned of the New England clergymen. After settling in Massachusetts he lead an exodus to Connecticut in 1635, where for the rest of his life he became the dominant figure. His departure from the Bay Colony did not imply any major break with Puritan orthodoxy. Hooker remained one of the leading spokesmen for the New England Way.

We must see it [sin] clearly in its own Nature, its Native color and proper hue: It's not every slight conceit, not every general and cursorie, confused thought or careless consideration that will serve the turn, or do the work here; we are all sinners; it is my infirmity, I cannot help it; my weakness, I cannot be rid of it; no man lives without faults and follies, the best have their failings; In many things we offend all. But alas all the wind shakes no Corn, it costs more to see sin aright than a few words, of course; It's one thing to say sin is thus and thus, another thing to see it to be such; we must look wisely and steddily upon our distempers, look sin in the face, and discern it to the full; the want whereof is the cause of our mistaking our estates, and not

SOURCE. Thomas Hooker, "Human Sin and the Disruption of Divine Order," from *The Application of Redemption by the Effectual Work of the Word and Spirit of Christ,* 2d Edition, London, 1659, pp. 53–63.

redressing of our hearts and ways, Gal. 6.4. "Let a man prove his own work." Before the Goldsmith can sever and see the Dross asunder from the Gold, he must search the very bowels of the Mettal, and try it by touch, by taste, by hammer and by fire; and then he will be able to speak by proof what it is; So here. We perceive sin in the crowd and by hearsay, when we attend some common and customary expressions taken up by persons in their common converse, and so report what others speak, and yet never knew the Truth, what either others or we say, but we do not single out our corruptions and survey the loathsomness of them, as they come naked in their own Natures; this we ought to do.

There is great odds betwixt the knowledg of a Traveller, that in his own Person hath taken a view of many Coasts, past through many Countries, and hath there taken up his abode some time, and by Experience hath been an Eye-Witness of the extreme cold, and scorching heats, hath surveyed the glory and beauty of the one, the barrenness and meanness of the other; he hath been in the Wars, and seen the ruin and desolation wrought there; and another that sits by his fireside, and happily reads the story of these in a Book, or views the proportion of these in a Map; the odds is great, and the difference of their knowledge more than a little: the one saw the Country really, the other only in the story; the one hath seen the very place, the other only in the paint of the Map drawn. The like difference is there in the right discerning of sin; the one hath surveyed the compass of his whole course, searched the frame of his own heart, and examined the windings and turnings of his own ways; he hath seen what sin is, and what it hath done, how it hath made havock of his peace and comfort, ruinated and laid waste the very Principles of Reason and Nature, and Morality, and made him a terror to himself, when he hath looked over the loathsom abominations that lie in his bosom, that he is afraid to approach the presence of the Lord to bewail his sins, and to crave pardon, lest he should be confounded for them, while he is but confessing of them; afraid and ashamed lest any man living should know but the least part of that which he knows by himself, and could count it happy that himself was not, that the remembrance of those hideous evils of his might be no more; Another happily hears the like preached or repeated, reads them writ or recorded in some Authors, and is able to remember and relate them. The odds is marvelous great. The one sees the History of sin, the other the Nature of it; the one knows the relation of sin as it is mapped out, and recorded; the other the poison, as by experience he hath found and proved it. It's one thing to see a disease in the Book, or in a mans body, another thing to find and feel it in a mans self. There is the report of it, here the malignity and venom of it.

But how shall we see clearly the Nature of sin in his naked hue?

This will be discovered and may be conceived in the Particulars following. Look we at it: First, As it respects God. Secondly, As it concerns ourselves. As it hath reference to God, the vileness of the nature of sin may thus appear.

It would dispossess God of that absolute Supremacy which is indeed his Prerogative Royal, and doth in a peculiar manner appertayn to him, as the Diamond of his Crown, and Diadem of his Deity, so the Apostle, "He is God over all blessed forever," Rom. 9.5. All from him and all for him, he is the absolute first being, the absolute last end, and herein is the crown of his Glory. All those attributes of Wisdom, Goodness, Holiness, Power, Justice, Mercy, the shine and Concurrency of all those meeting together is to set out the unconceivable excellency of his Glorious name, which exceeds all praise. "Thine is the Kingdom, the power and the glory;" the right of all and so the rule of all and the Glory of all belongs to him.

Now herein lies the unconceivable hainousness of the hellish nature of sin, it would justle the Almighty out of the Throne of his Glorious Soveraignty, and indeed be above him. For the will of man being the chiefest of all his workmanship, all for his body, the body of the soul, the mind to attend upon the will, the will to attend upon God, and to make choice of him, and his will, that is next to him, and he onely above that: and that should have been his Throne and Temple or Chair of State, in which he would have Set his Soveraignty forever. He did in an Especial manner intend to meet with man, and to communicate himself to man in his righteous Law, as the rule of his Holy and righteous will, by which the will of Adam should have been ruled and guided to him, and made happy in him; and all Creatures should have served God in man, and been happy by or through him, serving of God, being happy in him; But when the will went from under the government of his rule, by sin, it would be above God, and be happy without him, for the rule of the law in each command of it, holds forth a threefold expression of Soveraignty from the Lord, and therein the Soveraignty of all the rest of his Attributes.

1. The Powerful Supremacy of his just will, as that he hath right to dispose of all and authority to command all at his pleasure; "What if God will?" Rom. 9.22. "My counsel shall stand and I will do all my pleasure," Isa. 46.10. And as its true of what shall be done upon us, so his will hath Soveraignty of Command in what should be done by us; we are to say "the will of the Lord be done;" Davids warrant was "to do all Gods wills," Acts. 13.22., and our Saviour himself professeth, John. 6.38., "that he came not to do his own will but the will of him that sent him," and therefore his wrath and jealousie and judgment will break out in case that be disobeyed.

2. There is also a fulness of wisdom in the law of God revealed to guide and direct us in the way we should walk, Psal. 19.7., "the law of God makes wise the simple," 2. Tim. 3.15., "it's able to make us wise unto Salvation."

3. There's a Sufficiency of God to content and satisfy us. "Blessed are they who walk in his wayes, and blessed are they that keep his Testimonies." Psal. 119.1.2. "Great prosperity have they that love the law, and nothing shall offend them," ver. 16., and in truth there can be no greater reward for doing well, than to be enabled to do well; he that hath attayned his last end he cannot go further, he cannot be better.

Now by sin we justle the law out of its place, and the Lord out of his Glorious Soveraignty, pluck the Crown from his head, and the Scepter out of his hand, and we say and profess by our practice, there is not authority and power there to govern, nor wisdom to guide, nor good to content me, but I will be swayed by mine own will and led by mine own deluded reason and satisfied with my own lusts. This is the guide of every graceless heart in the commission of sin. . . .

Its a grievous thing to the loose person he cannot have his pleasures but he must have his guilt and gall with them; Its grievous to the worlding that he cannot lay hold on the world by unjust means, but Conscience layes hold upon him as breaking the law. Thou that knowest and keepest thy pride and stub-

borness and thy distempers, know assuredly thou dost justle God
out of the Thorne of his Glorious Soveraignty and thou dost
profess, Not Gods will but thine own (which is above his) shall
rule thee; thy carnal reason and the folly of thy mind is above
the wisdome of the Lord and that shall guide thee; to please
thine own stubborn crooked pervers spirit, is a greater good than
to please God and enjoy happiness, for this more Contents thee;
That when thou considerest but thy Course, dost thou not
wonder that the great and Terrible God doth not push such a
poor insolent worm to ponder, and send thee packing to the pitt
every moment.

It smites at the Essence of the Almighty, and the desire of the
sinner, is not only that God should not be supream but that
indeed he should not be at all, and therefore it would destroy
the being of Jehovah. Psal. 81.15., sinners are called "the haters
of the Lord." John. 15.24., "they hated both me and my Father."
Now he that hates endeavours if it be possible the annihilation
of the thing hated and its most certain were it in their power,
they would pluck God out of Heaven, the light of his truth out
of their Consciences, and the law out of the Societies and Assem-
blies where they live, that they might have elbow room to live
as they list. Nay what ever they hate most and intend, and plott
more evil against in all the world, they hate God most of all, and
intend more evil against him than against all their Enemies
besides, because they hate all for his sake, therefore wicked men
"are said to destroy the law," Psal. 126.119; the Adulterer loaths
that law that condemns uncleaness; the Earthworm would destroy that law that forbids Covetousness, they are sayd to hate
the light, John. 3.21., to hate the Saints and Servants of the Lord,
John. 15.18.; "the world hates you;" he that hates the Lantern for
the lights sake, he hates the light much more, he that hates the
faithful because of the Image of God, and the Grace that appears
there, he hates the God of all, Grace and Holiness, most of all,
so God to Zenacharib, Isa. 37.28: "I know thy going out and thy
Comming in, and thy rage against me." Oh it would be their
content, if there was no God in the world to govern them, no law
to curbe them, no justice to punish, no truth to trouble them.
Learn therefore to see how far your rebellions reach; It is not

arguments you gainsay, not the Counsel of a Minister you reject, the command of a Magistate ye oppose, evidence of rule or reason ye resist; but be it known to you, you fly in the very face of the Almighty, and it is not the Gospel of Grace ye would have destroyed, but the spirit of Grace, the author of Grace the Lord Jesus, the God of all Grace that ye hate.

It crosseth the whole course of Providence, perverts the work of the Creature and defaceth the beautiful frame, and that sweet correspondence and orderly usefulness the Lord first implanted in the order of things; The heavens deny their influence, the Earth her strength, the Corn her nourishment, thank sin for that. Weeds come instead of herbs, Cockle and Darnel instead of Wheat, thank sin for that, Rom. 8.22. "The whole Creature (or Creation) grones under vanity," either cannot do what it would or else misseth of that good and end it intended, breeds nothing but vanity, brings forth nothing but vexation; It crooks all things so as that none can straiten them, makes so many wants that none can supply them, Eccles. 1.15. This makes crooked Servants in a family, no man can rule them, crooked inhabitants in towns, crooked members in Congregations, there's no ordering nor joyning of them in that comly accord, and mutual subjection; know they said, "the adversary sin hath done all this." Man was the mean betwixt God and the Creature to convey all good with all the constancy of it, and therefore when Man breaks, Heaven and Earth breaks all asunder, the Conduit being cracked and displaced there can be no conveyance from the Fountain.

In regard of ourselves, see we and consider nakedly the nature of sin, in Four particulars.

Its that which makes a separation between God and the soul, breaks that Union and Communion with God for which we were made, and in the enjoyment of which we should be blessed and happie, Isai. 59.1.2., "Gods ear is not heavy that it cannot hear nor his hand that it cannot help, but your iniquities have separated betwixt God and you and your sins have hid his face that he will not hear for he professeth," Psal. 5.4., "that he is a God that wills not wickedness neither shall iniquity dwell with him. Into the new Jerusalem shall no unclean thing enter, but without shall be dogs," Rev. 21.27. The Dogs to their Kennel, and Hogs

to their Sty and Mire: but if an impenitent wretch should come
into Heaven, the Lord would go out of Heaven; Iniquity shall
not dwell with sin. That then that deprives me of my greatest
good for which I came into the world, and for which I live and
labor in the world, and without which I had better never to have
been born, nay that which deprives me of an universal good, a
good that hath all good in it, that must needs be an evil, but have
all evil in it: but so doth sin deprive me of God as the Object of
my will, and that wills all good, and therefore it must bring in
Truth all evil with it. Shame takes away my Honor, Poverty my
Wealth, Persecution my Peace, Prison my Liberty, Death my Life,
yet a man may still be a happy man, lose his Life, and live
eternally: But sin takes away my God, and with him all good
goes; Prosperity without God will be my Poyson, Honor without
him my bane; nay, the word without God hardens me, my endeavor without him profits nothing at all for my good. A Natural
man hath no God in any thing, and therefore hath no good.

It brings an incapability in regard to my self to receive good,
and an impossibility in regard to God himself to work my
spiritual good, while my sin Continues, and I Continue impenitent in it. An incapability of a spiritual blessing, "Why
transgress ye the Commandement of the Lord, that ye cannot
prosper do what ye can," 2 Chron. 24.20. And "He that being
often reproved hardens his heart, shall be consumed suddenly
and there is no remedy," He that spills the Physick that should
cure him, the meat that should nourish him, there is no remedy
but he must needs dye, so that the Commission of sin makes not
only a separation from God, but obstinate resistance and continuance in it, maintains an infinite and everlasting distance
between God and the Soul: So that so long as the sinful resistance
of thy soul continues, God cannot vouch-safe the Comforting and
guiding presence of his grace; because it's cross to the Covenant
of Grace he hath made, which he will not deny, and his Oath
which he will not alter. So that should the Lord save thee and
thy Corruption, carry thee and thy proud unbelieving heart to
heaven he must nullify the Gospel (Heb. 5.9. "He's the author of
Salvation to them that obey him") and forswear himself (Heb.
3.18. "He hath sworn unbeleevers shall not enter into his rest"),

he must cease to be just and holy, and so to be God.

As Saul said to Jonathan concerning David, 1 Sam. 20.30,31. "So long as the Son of Jesse lives, thou shalt not be established, nor thy Kingdom:" So do thou plead against thyself and with thy own soul; So long as these rebellious distempers continue, Grace and Peace, and the Kingdom of Christ can never be established in thy heart, For this obstinate resistance differs nothing from the plagues of the state of the damned, when they come to the highest measure, but that it is not yet total and final, there being some kind of abatement of the measure of it, and stoppage of the power of it. Imagine thou sawest the Lord Jesus coming in the clouds, and heardest the last trump blow, "Arise ye dead, and come to judgement." Imagine thou sawest the Judge of all the World sitting upon the Throne, thousands of Angels before him, and ten thousands ministring unto him, the Sheep standing on his right hand, and the Goats at the left; Suppose thou heardest that dreadful Sentence, and final Doom pass from the Lord of Life (whose Word made Heaven and Earth, and will shake both) "Depart from me ye cursed;" How would thy heart shake and sink, and die within thee in the thought thereof, wert thou really perswaded it was thy portion? Know, that by the dayly continuance in sin, thou dost to the utmost of thy power execute that Sentence upon thy soul; It's thy life, thy labor, the desire of thy heart, and thy daily practice to depart away from the God of all Grace and Peace, and turn the Tombstone of everlasting destruction upon thine own soul.

It's the cause which brings all other evils of punishment into the World, and without this they are not evil, but so far as sin is in them. The sting of a trouble, the poyson and malignity of a punishment and affliction, the evil of the evil of any judgement, it is the sin that brings it, or attends it, Jer. 2.19. "Thine own wickedness shall correct thee, and thy back slidings shall reprove thee, know therefore that it is an evil, and bitter thing that thou hast forsaken the Lord," Jer. 4.13. "Thy ways and doings have procured these things unto thee, therefore it is bitter, and reacheth unto the heart." Take miseries and crosses without sin, they are like to be without a sting, the Serpent without poyson, ye may take them ,and make Medicines of them. So Paul

1 Cor. 15.55., he playes with death itself, sports with the Grave. "Oh death, where is thy sting? Oh Grave where is thy Victory? The sting of death is sin." All the harmful annoyance in sorrows and punishments, further than either they come from sin, or else tend to it, they are rather improvements of what we have than parting with anything we do enjoy, we rather lay out our conveniences than seem to lose them, yea, they increase our Crown, and do not diminish our Comfort. "Blessed are ye when men revile you, and persecute you, and speak all manner of evil of you for my sake, for great is your reward in Heaven," Matth. 5.11. There is a blessing in persecutions and reproaches when they be not mingled with the deserts of our sins; yea, our momentary short affliction for a good cause, and a good Conscience, works an excessive exceeding weight of Glory. If then sin brings all evils, and makes all evils indeed to us, then is it worse than all those evils.

It brings a Curse upon all our Comforts, blasts all our blessings, the best of all our endeavors, the use of all the choicest of all Gods Ordinances; it's so evil and vile, that it makes the use of all good things, and all the most glorious, both Ordinances and Improvements evil to us. Hag. 2.13,14. When the question was made to the Priest: "If one that is unclean by a dead Body touch any of the holy things, shall it be unclean? And he answered, Yea. So is this People, and so is this nation before me, saith the Lord; and so is every work of their hands, and that which they offer is unclean." If any good thing a wicked man had, or any action he did, might be good, or bring good to him, in reason it was the Services and Sacrifices wherein he did approach unto God and perform Service to him, and yet "the Sacrifice of the wicked is an abomination to the Lord," Prov. 28.9., and Tit. 1.15., "To the pure all things are pure: but to the unbelieving there is nothing pure, but their very Consciences are defiled." It is a desperate Malignity in the temper of the Stomach, that should turn our Meat and diet into Diseases, the best Cordials and Preservatives into Poysons, so that what in reason is appointed to nourish a man should kill him. Such is the venom and malignity of sin, makes the use of the best things become evil, nay, the greatest evil to us many times; Psal. 109.7., "Let his prayer be turned into sin." That which is appointed by God to be the choicest means to prevent sin, is turned into sin out of the corrupt distemper of these carnal hearts of ours.

Hence then it follows; That sin is the greatest evil in the world, or indeed that can be. For, That which separates the soul from God, that which brings all evils of punishment, and makes all evils truly evil, and spoils all good things to us, that must needs be the greatest evil, but this is the nature of sin, as hath already appeared.

3   *Thomas Shepard*

Salvation by Covenant

Thomas Shepard, like his father-in-law Thomas Hooker, was one of the leading divines of New England. For many years he ministered to the congregation at Cambridge.

In the following selection Shepard expresses the hope, which the covenant of grace provided, that the abyss created by sin between God and man could be bridged. Out of his infinite graciousness God offered man a means of living with His frightening power. Through it men could hope to know, in some measure, the intentions of the unknowable God. Yet, as Shepard warns, it was necessary always to be wary lest one assume too much.

The blessed God hath evermore delighted to reveale and communicate himselfe by way of Covenant; he might have done good to man before his fall, as also since his fall, without binding himself in the bond of Covenant. Noah, Abraham, and David, Jewes, Gentiles might have had the blessings intended, without any

SOURCE. Thomas Shepard, "Salvation by Covenant," from "To the Reader," Preface to Peter Bulkeley, *The Gospel Covenant*, 2d Edition, London, 1651.

promise or Covenant; but the Lords heart is so full of love
(especially to his own) that it cannot be contained so long within
the bounds of secrecy, *viz.* from Gods eternall purpose to the
actuall accomplishment of good things intended, but it must
aforehand overflow and breake out into the many streames of a
blessed covenant; the Lord can never get near enough to his
people, and thinkes he can never get them near enough unto
himselfe, and therefore unites and binds and fastens them close
to himself, and himself unto them by the bonds of a Covenant.
And therefore when wee breake our Covenant, and that will not
hold us, he takes a faster bond, and makes a sure and everlasting
Covenant, according to grace, not according to workes, and that
shall hold his people firm unto himself, and hold himself close
and fast unto them, that he may never depart from us. Oh, the
depth of Gods grace herein, that when sinfull man deserves never
to have the least good word from him, that he should open his
whole heart and purpose to him, in a Covenant; that when he
deserves nothing else but separation from God, and to be driven
up and downe the world, as a Vagabond, or as dryed leaves, fallen
from our God, that yet the Almighty God cannot be content with
it, but must make himselfe to us, and us to himselfe more sure
and near then ever before! And is not this Covenant then
(Christian Reader) worth thy looking into and searching after?
Surely never was there a time wherein the Lord calls his people
to more serious searching into the nature of the Covenant, then
in these days. . . .

Is it not time for the people of God now to pry into the secret
of Gods Covenant (which he reveales to them that feare him,
Psal. 25.14) when by clipping of it, and distinguishing about it,
the beautiful countenance of it begins to be changed and transformed by those Angels of new light which once it had, when it
began to be published in the simplicity of it by the Apostles of
Christ, 2 Cor. 11.3. Nay, is not the time come, wherein the Lord
of hosts seemes to have a quarrell against all the world, and
especially his Churches and people, whom he goes on to waste
by the sharpest sword that (almost) was ever drawne out? and
is it not the duty of all that have but the least sparke of holy
feare and trembling, to aske and search diligently, what should

be the reason of this sore anger and hot displeasure, before they and theirs be consumed in the burning flames of it? Search the Scriptures, and there we shall find the cause, and see God himself laying his finger upon that which is the sore, & the wound of such times; for so it is said, Isa. 24.1 to 5, "Behold, the Lord maketh the earth empty and waste, and turnes it upside downe, and scattereth abroad the inhabitants thereof; and it shall be as with the people, so with the Priest; and the Land shall be utterly spoiled." Why? "For the earth is defiled under the Inhabitants thereof." Why so? "Because they have transgressed the Lawes, changed the Ordinance, and broken the Everlasting Covenant," and therefore when the Lord shall have wasted his Church, and hath made it as Adnab and Zeboim, when the heathen Nations shall aske, Wherefore hath the Lord done all this against this Land? what meaneth the heat of his great anger? The answer is made by the Lord himselfe expresly, Deut. 29.25 viz. "Because they have forsaken the Covenant of the Lord God of their fathers," Grace, they breake the league of peace between God and them-selves; and hence if acts of hostilitie in desolating Kingdoms, Churches, families and persons, breake out from a long-suffering God, they may easily see the cause; and that the cause and quarrell of God herein is just.

As all good things are conveyed to Gods people, not barely by common providence, but by speciall Covenants, Isa. 63.8,9, So all the evills they meet with in this world (if in them the face of Gods anger appeares) upon narrow search will be found to arise from breach of Covenant more or lesse. So that if it be the great Cause of all the publick calamities of the Church and people of God, and those calamities are already begun, and Gods hand is stretched out still, Was there then ever a more seasonable time and houre to study the Covenant, and so see the sin, repent of it, and at last to lay hold of Gods rich grace and bowels in it, lest the Lord go on and fulfill the word of his servants, and expose most pleasant lands to the doleful lamentation of a very little remnant, reserved as a few coales in the ashes, when all else is consumed. As particular persons when they breake their Cove-nant, the Lord therefore breaks out against them: So when whole

Churches forsake their Covenant, the Lord therefore doth sorely
visit them. Sins of ignorance the Lord Jesus pities, Heb. 5.2. and
many times winks at; but sins against light he cannot endure,
2 Pet. 2. 21. Sins against light are great, but sins against purpose
and Covenant, nay Gods Covenant, are by many degrees worse,
for the soule of man rusheth most violently and strongly against
God, when it breaks through all the light of the minde and purposes of the will, that stand in his way to keep him from sin; and
is not this done by breach of Covenant? And therefore no
wonder if the Lord makes his peoples chaine heavy by sore
affliction, until they come to consider and behold this sin, and
learne more fear (after they are bound to their good behaviour,)
of breaking Covenant with God againe.

It is true, the Covenant effectually made, can never really be
broke, yet externally it may. But suppose Gods Churches were
in greatest peace, and had a blessed rest from all their labours
round about them; yet what is the childes portion by his legacy
left him written with the finger of God his Father, in the new
Covenant, and the bloud of Jesus Christ his redeemer, in his last
Will and Testament? What is a Christians comfort, and where
doth it chiefly lie, but in this, That the Lord hath made with
him an everlasting Covenant, in all things established and sure?
Which were the last breathings of the sweet Singer of Israel, and
the last bubblings up of the joy of his heart, 2 Sam. 23.5. God the
Fathers eternall purposes are sealed secrets, not immediately
seene, and the full and blessed accomplishments of those purposes are not yet experimentally felt; the Covenant is the midst
between both Gods purposes and performances, by which and in
which we come to see the one, before the world began, and by
a blessed Faith (which makes things absent, present) to enjoy the
other, which shall be our glory, when this world shall be burnt
up, and all things in it shall have an end. For in Gods Covenant
and promise we see with open face Gods secret purpose for time
past. Gods purposes toward his people being as it were nothing
else but promises concealed, and Gods promises in the Covenant
being nothing else but his purposes revealed; as also in the same
Covenant and promises we see performances for future, as if they
were accomplishments at present. Where then is a Christians

comfort, but in that Covenant where in two Eternities (as it were) meet together and whereby he may see accomplishments (made sure to him) of eternall glory, arising from blessed purposes of eternall Grace? In a word, wherein he fastens upon God, and hath him from everlasting to everlasting, comprehended at hand neare & obvious in his words of a gracious Covenant?

PART TWO

Community Versus Calling

4
Bernard Bailyn
Puritan Social Ideals and the Dilemma of the New England Merchants

Professor Bernard Bailyn of Harvard University is one of the leading living historians of early America. He has written the most perceptive study of the colonial origins of American education and more recently brilliant works on the ideas of the American Revolution.

Bailyn's book, The New England Merchants in the Seventeenth Century, *is a subtle and complex account of the intellectual and social context of commercial activity in early Massachusetts. In the following selections he discusses the dilemma that confronted the Puritan merchants as they tried to pursue their legitimate calling without violating Puritan social ideals.*

The ethical keystone of the great edifice of Calvinism was the conviction that all men were totally responsible for their behavior. The heart of the question, as a sixteenth-century writer put it, is not the quantity of sin but the fact that God's majesty is offended at all; "... be the thing never so little, yet the breach of his Commandment deserveth death."

SOURCE. Reprinted by permission of the publishers from Bernard Bailyn, *The New England Merchants in the Seventeenth Century*, pp. 20–23, 39–44. Cambridge, Mass.: Harvard University Press, Copyright 1955 by the President and Fellows of Harvard College.

To men for whom life was moral experience, no actions were more relevant to the overwhelming consideration of salvation than those touching the welfare of one's fellow men. For, however discouraging to those who found a righteous life a simpler matter when lived in solitude, the Puritan's obligation to live intensively as a social being was nothing less than God's will. Society was an organism functioning for the good of all its members. Each component sought its own welfare, yet contributed and was subordinated to the whole. In a world of sinful men seeking salvation a compact society had the advantage of a readier discipline exerted by those in authority. This fact was of first importance, for men in positions of political power were, in their official capacities, limited agents of God. Those you have called to public office, Winthrop told a bumptious General Court, "have our authority from God, in way of an ordinance, such as hath the image of God eminently stamped upon it, the contempt and violation whereof hath been vindicated with examples of divine vengeance." Leaders, once selected, were to whip the moral sluggards into line, for their own good, for the welfare of society, and for the glory of God.

The variety of men's occupations made it possible for each individual to find the work in which he could best acquit himself of his obligations. But it also meant that some men were more exposed to temptation than others. Those whose work bore broadly on the welfare of others were called upon to exert a scrupulousness in their transactions commensurate with the temptation to sin. Of all private occupations trade was morally the most dangerous.

The soul of the merchant was constantly exposed to sin by virtue of his control of goods necessary to other people. Since proof of the diligence he applied in his calling was in the profits he made from precisely such exchanges, could a line be drawn between industry and avarice? The Puritans answered, as had Catholics for half a millenium, that it could, and they designated this line the "just price."

They assumed that there existed an ideal standard of valuation applicable to every situation. An unjust figure was the result not so much of the mechanical operation of an impersonal market as of some individual's gluttony. A just charge was one willingly paid by a person experienced in such matters and in need of the article but under no undue compulsion to buy. The Reverend John Cotton laid out the principles clearly: "A man may not sell above the current price, i.e., such a price as is usual in the time and place, and as another (who knows the worth of the commodity) would give for it, if he had occasion to use it. . ." A merchant's personal losses or misfortunes ought never to be reflected in an increased valuation, "but where there is a scarcity of the commodity," Cotton wrote, "there men may raise their price; for now it is a hand of God upon the commodity, and not the person." As for the particular determination of the price, in case private men cannot agree on a common estimate, "the governor, with one or more of the councell" or perhaps "certaine select men" will be able to make the matter clear. Convinced that justice could be reached, the Puritans sought only the detailed figures in concrete situations.

Equally treacherous to the soul of the businessman and the good of the public was the fact that the merchants came into control of the available supply of money and charged interest on debts. One who controlled supplies of cash or credit held a knife over a vital vein in the social body. Such a power had for centuries required the closest regulation, which it had duly received along with its rationalization in the literature on usury. But in the sixteenth century the medieval excoriation of all interest-bearing loans had given way to a qualified acceptance of interest within the limits of justice and official determination. The New England Puritans took over the continental Calvinist phrasing of this acceptance. The principle was clear. "What rule must wee observe in lending?" asked Winthrop rhetorically.

ANS: Thou must observe whether thy brother hath present or probable, or possible meanes of repayeing thee, if ther be none of these, thou must give him according to his necessity, rather then lend him as hee requires; if he hath present meanes of repayeing thee, thou art to looke at him, not as an Act of mercy, but by way of Commerce, wherein thou arte to walke by the rule of Justice. . . If any of thy brethren be poore etc. thou shalt lend

him sufficient that men might not shift off this duty by the
apparent hazzard. . . From him that would borrow of thee turne
not away.

QUEST: What rule must wee observe in forgiveing?

ANS: Whether thou didst lend by way of Commerce or in mercy,
if he have noething to pay thee [thou] must forgive him (except
in cause where thou hast a surety or a lawfull pleadge) Deut. 15.2.

John Cotton, flourishing *"Exo. 22. 25. Lev. 25. 35, 36,"* asserted
quite simply: "Noe increase to be taken of a poore brother or
neighbour for anything lent unto him."

Though church and state in New England most readily im-
pinged on the professional life of the merchant in regard to just
price and usury, the assumption of justified control of economic
life had a far wider applicability. If prices came under the aegis
of authority so also did wages. Encouragement, even direct sub-
sidization of economic activity, no less than restriction, flowed
from the same obligation to manipulate material life for spiritual
ends.

Such precepts had a special appeal to a predominantly agri-
cultural people whose emigration was at least in part due to economic distress. Many settlers had lost their stability in a rapidly
changing world where "trades are carried soe deceiptfully and
unrightusly as that is almost inpossible for a good upright man to
maynteyne his charge and to live comfortably in his profession."
The Reverend John White, who had inspired the founding of
two commercial companies, voiced a typical thought in writing
to Winthrop,

"I heare shopkeeping begins to growe into request amongst
you. In former age all kinde of retailing wares (which I confess
is necessary for mens more convenient supply) was but an ap-
pendixe to some handicraft and to that I should reduce it if I
were to advise in the government. Superfluity of Shopkeepers
Inholders etc. are great burthens to any place. We in this Towne
where I live . . . are of my knowledg at Charge 1000*li* per annum
in maintaining several familys in that Condition, which we might
well spare for better employments wherein their labours might

produce something for the common good which is not furthered by such as drawe only one from another and consequently live by the sweat of other mens brows, producing nothing themselves by their owne endevours."

At a time when mercantilism in Europe made the needs of trade a reason of state some of these ideas of the New England leaders were archaic. Yet they were able to survive and even to flourish because the governing Fathers, being, in John Hull's phrase, "no babes nor windyheaded men," understood necessity to found their society on a solid economic base. They merely insisted that the life of business be placed within a structure whose proportions had been drawn by the hand of God.

These ideas were put into use in the very first years of the Puritan settlements and helped shape the development of institutions and traditions from the start. Nowhere else did Calvinist doctrines of social ethics find such full application. In Geneva, Scotland, and the Netherlands theory had always to be qualified to some extent by pre-Calvinist practices. In New England doctrine literally preceded practice.

.   .   .   .

In social origins the transplanted London tradesmen were unique among the settlers. Most of the colonists had known only life on the land, either as gentlemen, independent farmers, tenants, or laborers; consequently, both the magistrates and the majority of the population brought with them the attitudes and desires of rural Englishmen. To them land meant not so much wealth as security and stability, tradition and status. Shaken out of their familiar ways by economic and political disturbances, caught up in varying degrees by the cause of religious reform, most of the 20,000 Englishmen who migrated to America in the 1630's sought to recreate the village and farm life they had known. They accepted and probably welcomed the medieval social teaching of orthodox Puritanism if only for its inspiring support of the idea of the close-knit community that existed for the good of all its members and in which each man was his brother's keeper.

For the merchants, bred in London and the bustling outports, these needs and ideas were less urgent. The great metropolis was a hothouse of new values and attitudes. In contrast to that of the average agriculturist, the life pattern of merchants who, like Thomas Savage and Robert Keayne, could boast of having received "no portion from my parents or friends to begin the world withal," and, after a career of constant striving, having emerged triumphant from financial losses "sufficient to have broken the backe of any one man in the Country"—such life patterns were characterized by geographical and social mobility. To such men the authoritarianism of Winthrop's government, which suggested security and status to most of the settlers, tended to imply constriction and denial. Freed from the complexities and competition of the Old World cities and trained in some aspect of the production and distribution of goods, the merchants experienced a release of energies in America which frequently struck the Puritan leaders as brashness and insubordination. Conflict between men who had risen through the struggles of city life and the leaders of the Puritan Commonwealth was implicit from the start.

Yet the right of the merchants to participate fully in the community life was not challenged. All of them were received into a church and made freemen of the corporation. The difficulty took the form of a series of clashes between the merchants and the public authorities. Some of these were trivial and easily handled by the usual processes of law. Others led through subtle ways to serious trouble. In a society where theology and political theory were interwoven thin lines of doctrine were often the threads upon which rested the justification for the use of power. Dissatisfaction with the magistracy stemming from different assumptions as to the right of self-expression, political and economic as well as religious, could be voiced in hair-splitting theological disputes. One such controversy threatened to sever the Boston merchants from the rest of the community.

The "Antinomian schism" of 1636-1637 which rocked the Bay Colony to its foundations turned on the relative importance of inner, direct religious experience and conformity to the Calvinist laws of behavior in the attainment of a Christian life. The magistracy steadfastly maintained that conformity to the letter of the law, careful performance of religious duties, was essential discipline and that it should be evident in one before he was to be admitted to church membership. To them the dissenters were dangerous mystics whose belief in the prior importance of spiritual illumination was not only a doctrinal heresy but also a threat to civil and ecclesiastical polity.

The merchants, with striking uniformity, backed the dissenters. The challenge centered in the person of Anne Hutchinson, whose husband, son, and brother-in-law were among the most prominent early merchants. Her party was composed predominantly of inhabitants of Boston, already the main seat of New England commerce. Among her adherents considered dangerous enough to be disarmed by the General Court were William, Richard, and Edward Hutchinson, Edward Rainsford, Thomas Savage, Robert Harding, Richard Parker, Edward Bendall, and John Coggeshall. Most of these merchant heretics left Massachusetts for the exile of Rhode Island, either with the Hutchinsons to Portsmouth or with William Coddington to Newport. The "Antinomian schism" uprooted some of the most flourishing merchants of Boston and prepared the soil of Rhode Island for the growth of a commercial community.

The divergence between the merchants and most of the rest of the Puritan population manifested itself more explicitly in public condemnations for malpractices in trade, particularly overcharging, usury, taking advantage of a neighbor's need. The public clamor that accompanied one such incident grew to such proportions as to indicate that an important source of discontent had been touched.

Robert Keayne was a typical self-made tradesman of London. Starting as a butcher's son in Windsor, he had risen through apprenticeship in London to prominence as a merchant tailor. Transplanted to New England in 1635, he was received into the church, made a freeman of the corporation, and immediately assumed a leading position in local affairs. He moved into a house and shop on the southwest corner of Cornhill and King streets in the heart of Boston, one lot distant from the First Church and facing the central market square. Drawing on the "two or 3000 lb in good estate" he had brought with him, he reëstablished contact with his London friends and commenced his career as a retailer of imported manufactures. For four years he rode the wave of the inflation, selling badly needed goods to the immigrants for whatever prices he could get. But in November 1639 he was struck down by both church and state. Keayne was charged in General Court with "taking above six-pence in the shilling profit; in some above eight-pence; and in some small things, above two for one."

It had all started with a bag of nails he had sold at what he claimed was a perfectly reasonable price. Once this single charge had exposed the merchant to public censure, a variety of other accusations, such as overcharging for "great gold buttons," a bridle, and a skein of thread, were fired at him. Haled before the highest court he was made to face a barrage of denunciation. So agonizing were the resulting wounds that in drawing up his Last Will and Testament fourteen years later he referred again and again to the incident as if to ease the pain of that "deepe and sharpe censure that was layd upon me in the Country and carryed on with so much bitterness and indignation... contrary or beyond the quality and desert of the complaynts that came against me." The public ire was expressed not so much in the court's conviction of the merchant as in the fact that the fine was fixed at no less the £200. But even that was cheap considering the state of public feeling. Keayne later wrote that "if some could have had their wills they would have had the fyne mounted up to 1000lb yea 500lb was too little except some coporal punishment was added to it, such as my mans [sic] standing openly on a market day with a Bridle in his mouth or at least about his necke, as I was credibly informed. Here was well guided zeale."

So far only the civil sword had struck. The church then took up the matter. The elders studied "how farr I was guilty of all those claymors and rumors that then I lay under," and exposed his defense to a most "exquisite search." Though he escaped excommunication, a fact he later boasted of, he was given a severe admonition "... in the Name of the Church for selling his wares at excessive Rates, to the Dishonor of Gods name, the Offence of the Generall Cort, and the Publique scandall of the Cuntry." It took a "penetentiall acknowledgment" of his sin to regain full membership in the church.

To Keayne the most painful part of this episode (and also of his more famous involvement three years later with Goody Sherman and her sow) was not the fine or the admonition but the public insistence that he was a sinner.

". . . the newnes and straingnes of the thing, to be brought forth into an open Court as a publique malefactor, was both a shame and an amazement to me. It was the greife of my soule (and I desire it may ever so be in a greater measure) that any act of mine (though not justly but by misconstruction) should be an occasion of scandall to the Gospell and profession of the Lord Jesus, or that my selfe should be looked at as one that had brought any just dishonor to God (which I have endeavored long and according to my weake abilitie desired to prevent) though God hath beene pleased for causes best knowne to himselfe to deny me such a blessing, and if it had beene in my owne power I should rather have chosen to have perished in my cradle than to have lived to such a time."

The merchant was as devout a Christian by his lights as his brother-in-law, the Reverend John Wilson. He had dedicated himself to the life of the spirit in the most befitting way. Not only had he been regular in his church attendance but he had kept notes on the sermons he had heard that he might refer to them later. He had studied the sacred books far into the night and left as the fruit of his labor "3 great writing bookes which are intended as an Exposition or Interpretation of the whole Bible . . . as also a 4th great writing booke which is an exposition on the Prophecy of Daniel, of the Revelations and the Prophecy of Hosea . . . all which Bookes are written with my owne hand . . . and worth all the paines and labour I have bestowed upon them, so that if I had 100lb layd me downe for them, to deprive me of them, till my sight or life should be taken of me I should not part from them." He had followed the Calvinist precepts of personal conduct. Never had he indulged in "an idle, lazie, or dronish life" or allowed himself "many spare hours to spend unprofitably away or to refresh myself with recreations." Naturally, he had prospered despite all the malice of his adversaries.

Finding evidence in the social teachings of Calvinism for the rectitude of his life, he could impute only sinfulness to those who attempted to blacken his name. But his enemies also drew upon religious ideas for the justification of their attack. To them it seemed clear that by all the relevant Calvinist standards of justice in business Keayne had sinned. In his scramble for profit he had trampled underfoot the notion of a just price. He had dealt with his debtors usuriously. He had put the increase of his own wealth above the common good. No amount of public benefaction could make up for such evil practices.

The original charge against the distraught merchant fell like a spark into an incendiary situation. The settlers, predisposed to believe middlemen parasites, found themselves utterly dependent on them for the most essential goods and equipment. Incapable of understanding or controlling the workings of the economy, they sought to attribute the cause of the soaring prices and the shortage of goods to human malevolence. Instances of merchants taking advantage of the situation confirmed them in their belief that only the most rigorous discipline of the businessmen could save them from misery. In the same Calvinist social teachings that had justified his life to Keayne they had a grammar for the translation of economics into morality, and in the machinery of the Puritan church and state a means of effecting these ideas. From the same texts the Puritan magistrates and the merchants read different lessons. The former learned the overwhelming importance of the organic society which subordinated the individual to the general good. Keayne learned the righteousness of those individual qualities whose secondary but attractive virtue it was to aid in the fight for success in business. Keayne's advice to the "Reverend Eldrs of this Country" that they "be as easily perswaded to yeeld in civill and earthly respects and things as they expect to prevayl with any of us when they have a request to make of us" would have implied to Winthrop the severance of the moral sinews in the body of Puritan society.

Keayne's Last Will and Testament expresses the dilemma of the first Puritan import merchants. Its 50,000 words were written under the compulsive need to gain final approval from a gen-

eration that seemed to confuse diligence with avarice. To be
both a pious Puritan and a successful merchant meant to live
under what would seem to have been insupportable pressures. It
meant to extend to the life of business a religious enthusiasm
which must be continuously dampened lest it singe the corners
of another's life. It meant to accumulate as much wealth as one
righteously could, only to dispose of it, like a steward, according
to the principle *uti non frui*. It demanded against the natural
desire to live spontaneously and heedlessly the total rationalization of life. Above all, it required an amount of self-discipline
that only great faith could sustain.

5   *John Robinson*

Diligent Labor and the Use of God's Creatures

*The Puritans believed firmly in the virtue of hard work and the right
to enjoy the fruits of honest labor. In the diligent pursuit of a proper
calling it was permissible for men to obtain riches, but seeking wealth
was frought with spiritual dangers. A man must not try to increase his
stock of the things of this world for their own sake. He must acknowledge that all his possessions come to him not merely as the product of
his own labor, but also as a blessing from God, a blessing that carried
with it the obligation to use his gains for the good of others as well as
for his own.*

*John Robinson was the spiritual father of the Plymouth colony. Al-
though he never set foot in America himself, his followers who came
over on the* Mayflower *brought his teachings to the New World. Although Robinson was, like the settlers in Plymouth, a moderate sepa-
ratist, he was highly regarded by the Massachusetts fathers. Robinson's
attitudes toward the calling and the problem of living in this world
while not being of it were not different from those of the Bay Colony
leaders.*

SOURCE. John Robinson, "Diligent Labor and the Use of God's Creature,"
from *Observations of Knowledge and Virtue* (n.p. 1625), pp. 143–147, 149–154,
157–162.

OF LABOUR, AND IDLENESS

God, who would have our first father, even in innocency, and
being Lord of the whole world, to labour (though without payne
or wearisomness) in dressing the Garden, and when he had
sinned, to eat his bread with the sweat of his brows, would have
none of his sinfull posteritie lead their life in Idleness; no nor
without exerciseing themselvs diligently in some lawfull calling,
or other. I say diligently: For as poore men play for recreation,
now and then, so do rich men work. But that sufficeth not. For
God who hath in the naturall body appointed unto every member its office, and function, which it is constantly to exercise,
would have no member in any societie, or body of men ordinarily
unimployed. Neyther doth that man (how great, or rich soever)
keep a good conscience before God, who makes labour but an
accessorie, and not a principall, and that which takes up his
ordinarie tyme.

Man is borne to sore labour, in body, or minde, as the spark
to fly upward. In heaven is onely rest without labour: in hell,
restless payn and torment: and as sin makes the earth (which is
between both) liker to hell, then heaven, so God for sin hath
given to the sons of man sore travail to afflict them upon earth.
And that in most wise, and gratious providence, considering the
mischeifs that come by idleness as: The weakning of the endowments of nature, whereas labour brings strength to the body,
and vigour to the mynde: yea the consumption of grace, as rust
consumes the iron for want of using. Yea, whereas idleness brings
bodily poverty like an armed man, it brings not onely spiritual
povertie in graces with it, but withall, a legion of vices, like so
many armed divels, puffing up the flesh with pride, and makeing
the heart Sathans anvile (who is commonly least idle, when men
are most) whereon to forge a thowsand vanities, and sinfull lusts,
as having a fit opportunity to perswade men to do evill, when
he findes them doing nothing; that so they, who will not sweat
in earth, eyther with the labour of the hand, or heart, (though
king Alphonsus sayd that God, and nature had given kings hands
as well as other men) might sweat in hell: and that if they will
not bear their part in the payns of men, they might partake in

the payns of the Devils. Whereas, on the contrary, if we do that which is good, and well done, though with labour, and payne-fulnes, the Labour is soon over, and gone, whereas the goodness and reward therof remayns behinde.

Proud folk despise Labour, and them that use it. And so it would be thought by many, far meaner than Josephs brethren, a disgracefull question to be asked, as they were by Pharaoh, Of what occupation they were? And this difference I have observed, for the matter in hand, that whereas in plentifull countryes, such as our own, it is half a shame to Labour, in such others, as wherein art and industry must supply natures defects, as in the country where I have last lived, it is a shame for a man not to work, and exercise himself in some one or other lawfull vocation. And in truth, there is more comfort to a good man in that which he gets, or saves by his labour, and providence, and Gods blessing thereupon, then in that which comes to him any other way. For he considers it not onely as a fruit of Gods love, but withall, as a reward of his obedience unto Gods commandement of labour and travayl to be undergone in this world of the children of men. It is a blessing upon every one that feareth the Lord, and walks in his wayes, that he shall eat the labour of his hands. And, he that without his own labour eyther of body or mynde, eats the labour of other mens hands onely, and lives by their sweat, is but like unto lice, and such other vermine. Let every godly Christian, in his place, say with Christ, "I must work the works of him that sent me, while it is day; the night cometh when no man can work...."

It is a great blessing, when God gives a man grace, and wisdom to take payns about things first lawfull, and secondly profitable. The diligent in evill are but like the devill, who compasseth the earth, and that like a roaring lyon, seeking whom he may devour. Such do best, when they do least. The life of others is *inquieta inertia*, busying, and oft times troubling both themselves, and others, with things altogether unprofitable, like the kings of Egypt in building their Pyramides, to the mispending of their own mony, and peoples labour. I have known divers, that with the tithe of the study, and payns taken by them, had it been rightly improved, and to profitable uses, might have benefited both themselvs, and others far more, then they have done, with all their diligence, and that with good meaning also.

Labour spent upon things eternall must not be counted lost, or too much, seeing temporall things of any worth are not usually obteyned without it. And surely, if heaven, and happiness could be had with so litle payns and trouble, as the world reckons, it were strange, if they were worth the haveing. And yet how many might obteyn the pearl of Christ promised with lesse payns, then they take for earthly and transitory things, which yet oft times they are disappointed of? Yea, I add, then many take for hell, which their wickedness brings upon them unavoydably? "Labour not for the meat which perisheth: but for that meat, which endureth unto eternall life," sayth Christ our Lord.

OF CALLINGS

The effectuall calling of a Christian is that by which the Lord first differenceth actually, and in the person himself, the elect from the reprobate, and by which the called approacheth, and draweth nigh unto God that calleth him, and that takes away his sin, which separated betweene the Lord, and him, both by justifying, and sanctifying him.

This generall calling of a Christian is incomparably more excellent, and honourable, then any particular calling, and state whatsoever. By it we are blessed with all spiritual blessings in heavenly things both for grace, & glory. It alone is properly an holy calling, hallowing all other callings, which also are so far lawfull, and lawfully used, as they further it, and not otherwise. If the excellency of it were well weighed, & rightly prized, no man honoured therewith should be thought worthy to be despised for any other meannesse, nor without it to be envyed for any other excellency how glorious soever in the worlds eye.

.   .   .   .

A lawfull calling is necessarie for every lawfull work: the generall calling of a Christian, before we can perform any Christian work aright, and so a particular calling to this, or that state of life, before we perform the works thereof. The inward calling is requisite in regard of God, who knows the inwards of the man, and with what heart, and affection he undertakes any state, or action: so is the outward also, because God is the God of order. Also, when a man knows himself to be orderly called to a condition of life, he both sets himself more chearfully, and roundly to the works thereof, wherein he is assured he servs Gods providence by his order, and appoyntment, and with fayth expects a blessing from God upon his endeavors in that course of life, in which his hand hath set him, and with all, bears with comfort the crosses befalling him therein: as wee see in David, whose sheild of comfort against all darts of danger was that God had selected him unto himself, and annoynted him his king upon Sion the mountayn of his holyness.

Little account is made by many of a lawfull outward calling; whereas indeed it is that alone, by which all states (save those that are naturall, and so are subject neyther to election nor change) are both constituted, and continued. For what makes him, who yesterday was none, to day to be a magistrate in the common wealth, minister in the Church, steward in the family, or any other officer, or member in any orderly society, but an orderly outward calling by them, who have lawfull authority to confer that state upon him? This being neglected opens a gap to all confusion in all states. The gifts of a man enable him to his office; his grace sanctifyes both the gifts, and office to the person; his inward calling perswades his heart to undertake the outward in desire to glorify God, and in love to men; his execution of it in the works thereof presuppose it, and testify his faythfulness in it: but onely the outward orderly calling confers the outward state, and condition of life.

Abilitie for a mans calling is greatly to be desired for many reasons. For, first, it is a thing well-pleasing in Gods sight, specially in the most serviceable courses of life, as we may see in Salomon, who being called to the state of a King, desired above all other things, kingly endowments, and therein pleased God greatly. Secondly, He whom God calls to a place, or sets over a business, he enables accordingly, as he did the same Salomon, being set over a people many in number, as the sand by the sea shore, with wisdom, and largeness of heart, as the sand by the sea shore. Thirdly, It is great ease to a man, when he is master of his place, and course, and able to play with it; otherwise, if he be compelled to strive continually with it, it will both make his life burthensome, and force him at some time, or other, to let fall the works thereof, as unable to weild it. Yet if such a one be willing, and able to bear it out, it is a good way for him to grow to great perfection, by daily improving his abilitie to the full: as Milo by using to bear a calf every day, proved able to bear him, when he was grown an oxe. Fourthly, It is an honour to a man to be excellent in his faculty, yea though it be mean in it self. And so men excelling in mean trades, or callings are more regarded, then those who are mean in more excellent faculties. One sayth truly, that "even plowmen and sheep-heards being excellent are applauded." Lastly, the unskilfulness of the artisan dishonours the art it self how excellent soever, in the eyes of many, although in reason it should not so be, seeing that the more excellent any profession is, it finds the fewer, whose worth can answer its excellencie.

Although callings most usefull, and necessarie, are most despised by prowd folks, both because they are ordinary and common, and followed by mean, and ordinary persons: yet it stands with a good conscience to provide, that our course of life be such, as in which we benefit humayne societyes. And an uncomfortable thing it is to him, that hath any either feare of God, or love to men, to spend his dayes, and labour in such a course, as by which more hurt then good comes to the world.

It is a good and godly course for a person diligently to read, and seriously to meditate upon such places of holy Scripture, as concern his, or her speciall calling: as, for the minister 1.Tim.3. and so for husband, and wife, father, and childe, master and servant, and the rest, that by so doing we may both more fully learn, and better remember, and conscionably practice the particular dutyes in which God would have us exercise our generall christian graces.

OF THE USE, AND ABUSE OF THINGS

We are said to enjoy God alone, and to use the creatures, because we are not to rest in them, but in God onely, to whom we are to be beholden by them. And of the things which we use, some of them we must use, as though we used them not: others, as though we used them. The World, and all things serving for this life, we ought to use with a kinde of indifferency, and without setting the affections of our hearts upon it, or them, how busy soever our hands be about them; spirituall good things, on the contrary, and which concerns our eternall happiness, we ought to use, as using them indeed, with all earnest bent of affection upon them, and as not suffering our selvs, at any hand, to be disappoynted of the fruit of them.

God (sayeth the wise man) "hath made every thing beautifull in his time;" and indeed, every thing is good for something; (I mean every thing that God hath made, for there are many vayn and lewd devises of men, which are truly good for nothing) as, on the other side, nothing is good for every thing. And hereupon Promethemus told the Satyre, when he would have kissed the fire, upon his first seeing it, that if he did so, it would burn his lips, as not being for that use, but to minister heat, and light. Some things alwayes bear, as it were, their use on their backs, and cause also the right use of other things, where they are found, as the sanctifying graces of Gods spirit, which yet some use more fully, and faythfully then others, and this is also a grace of God: whereas all other things have theyr good in theyr useing, and not in their owning. And a great poynt of wisdom, and advantage for good it is to apply things to their right use, and end, whether great, or final. He that can do this spiritually, is happy, though he have receaved but one pound for others five, or ten, As on the other side, how many were, (though not happy, yet) lesse miserable, if they altogether wanted the wit, learning, riches, and authority, which they want grace to use, according to the will of the giver?

A man hath that most, and best, whereof he hath the (lawfull) use. And hereupon a follower of a great Lord was wont to say, that he had, in effect, as much, as his Lord, though he were owner of little, or nothing, considering how he had the use of his gardens, and galleryes, to walk in, heard his musick, with as many ears, as he did, hunted with him in his parkes, and ate, and drank of the same, that he did, though a little after him, and so for the most other delights which his Lord enjoyed. And, in truth, what great difference is there, save in the proud, and covetous minde of a man, whether he himself, or another be owner of the good things, whereof he with him hath the lawfull use, and benefit?

Distinction must be put between the things themselves, and their casuall, and personall abuses; otherwise the natures of the things can neither be rightly conceaved of, nor expressed. Neyther doth the abuse of good things so take away, or make forfeyture of the use, as that the counsayl of Lycurgus is to be followed, who would have the vines cut down, because men were sometimes drunken with the grapes. Yet may the abuse of a thing be so common, and notorious, and the use so small, or needlesse, as better want the small use, then be in continuall danger of the great abuse of it.

The best things abused become the worst, both naturally, and morally, by reason of a greater force in them then in other things, which we must not therefore superstitiously disavow, or cease to account the best, as they are; but we must thereby be warned to use them the more warily, that we may enjoy their full goodness, and not prejudice them by abuse....

All evil stands in the abuse of good. And good things are abused commonly, eyther when they are unmeasurably used; as it is said of wyne, that the first cupp quenches thirst, the second procures chearfulness, the third drunkenness, and the fourth madness; or by applying them unaptly, or to the wrong ends, or persons: as when one offers light to the blynde, or speech to him that is deaf, or wisdom to a brutish man; or as when cowards fight with their tongues, and swash-bucklers dispute with their swords: or in regard of their supernaturall use, when we referre not all to the glory of God, and our own, and others eternall good, and welfare, which are the utmost ends of all things.

OF RICHES, AND POVERTY

The blessing of the Lord maketh rich. If wealth come by inheritance, it is Gods blessing that a man is borne of rich friends, and not of beggars; if by mens free gift, it is his blessing, that hath made them able, and willing to do us good. If goods be gotten by industry, providence, and skill, it is Gods blessing that both gives the faculty, and the use of it, and the successe unto it. And as riches are in themselvs Gods blessings, so are we to desire them of him, and to use lawfull diligence to get them, for the comfortable course of our naturall and civil state. For though we are to be able to bear poverty if God send it, yet should we rayther desire riches, as a man, though he can go afoot, yet will rayther chuse to ride. Secondly, to free us from such temptations unto sin, as povertie puts many upon. Thirdly, that they may minister unto us, and ours, more plentifull matter of exercising vertue, and goodness, specially of mercy towards the poore, and them in need. God could, if he would, eyther have made mens states more equall, or have given every one sufficient of his own, But he hath rayther chosen to make some rich, and some poore, that one might stand in need of another, and help another, that so he might try the mercy, and goodness of them that are able, in supplying the wants of the rest. And the richer sort that make not this account, know not wherefore God hath given them theyr goods, and are as poore in grace, as rich in the world.

Both poverty and riches, if they be in any extreamity, have their temptations, and those not small. . . . And, in truth, the middle state is freest from the greatest danger eyther of sin, or misery, in the world. . . . And of the two states, the wise man insinuates in that his prayer to the Lord, that the temptations of riches are the more dangerous. Povertie may drive a man to steale, or deal unjustly with others, and after to lye, or, it may be, and, as the Holy Ghost insinuates, by swearing to take the name of God in vain, to cover it. But if a man be rich, and full, he is in danger to deny God, and to say in pride, and contempt of him in effect as Pharoah did, who is the Lord? For hardly doth any thing cause the mynd to swell more with pryde, then riches, both by reason of the ease, and plenty of wordly good things,

which they bring with them: as also of the credit, which rich
men, or their purses, have in the world, and both those specially,
if they have gotten their wealth by their own art, or industrie.

He that is proud in a poore estate, would in a rich be intoller-
able before men, as he is in the meane while abhominable in
Gods sight. He that is humble in a prosperous, is a good scholler
of Christ, and hath taken out a hard lesson, which the Apostle
would have Timothy to charge the rich withall; which is, that
they should "not be high minded, nor trust in uncertayn riches."
From rich mens pride in themselves ariseth commonly contempt
of others, specially of the poore. I have known Nabals, who, in
my conscience, have, thought, that all that were not rich, were
fools, not withstanding any eminencie in them of gifts, or graces.

But thus to mock, or despise the poore, is to reproach God
that made him so; and besides, if the person be wise, and godly,
as he may well be, for any bar that his povertie puts against him,
it is withall, to despise the image of Gods wisdom, and goodness
in him. But for us, considering how the truly wise, by the
spirit of God pronounceth, that "the poore who walketh in his
uprightness, is better then he that is perverse in his way though
rich," as also, that "a poore, and wise child is better then an
old, and foolish king," we should have that strength of fayth
against sense, and carnall reason, as, in all resolvedness, to prefer
an honest, or wise poore man before a rich Naball. Besides,
though still the rich man be, and will be wise in his own eyes,
yet the poore that hath understanding searcheth him out; and
by searching often findes, that little witt (being imployed wholy
thereabout) and less grace, servs to get wealth with. . . .

God sends poverty upon men to humble them, both in the
want of bodily comforts, and specially in regard of the contempt,
which it ever casts upon men in the worlds eye. And blessed
indeed are they, who by povertie, and other worldly crosses are
humbled so, as to become poore in spirit. . . . Some are of opinion,
that none but rich folks can be proud. But the pride of many
(as was said of Diegenes) "may be seen through their rags."
And who ever saw any prouder, then some such worms, as in
whom no others could discern any thing outward or inward,
(saving the divell) that should make them so? God in his good,

and wise providence many tymes sends poverty, and other calamities upon such, to restreyn them, whose overswelling of pride, if they enjoyed a prosperous state, would make them both odious, and troublesome to all societies.

There be some, who out of a kynde of naturall diligence, patience, parsimony, and contentment with mean things, seem so fitted for a poore, and mean state, as that if they were ever pressed with want, they would ever be good, and vertuous, but being rich, and wealthy, are eyther base mynded, or arrogant, in the eyes of all men. There are also, [those] who by their kynde, and courteous disposition seem so fitted for prosperitie and plentie, that if they ever enjoyed it, they would be no meanly good people; and yet falling into a poore, and needie condition, they appear not onely impatient, but unconscionable also. But the truth is, that howsoever some be fitter for the one estate then the other, and so carry it better to the world, yet he that is not, in his measure, fit for eyther, is indeede fit for neyther. The Apostle had learned, and so must all good Christians with him, both to be full, and to be hungry, both to abound, and to suffer need. He that is not faithful in a little, would not be faythfull in a great deal; and so, for the contrary. He that is impatient, or unhonest in poverty, would be and is wanton, or arrogant, or otherwise faultie, though more closely, in aboundance; neyther is any broken with an afflicted state, save he, who is too much inveigled with a prosperous. He again, whose course is either to high, or too low, in plentie, would never keep a mean in want.

The over-valuation of riches drives divers men to divers, yea contrarie appearances: some to make themselves rich, though they have nothing: and others, to make show of poverty, though they have all aboundance. The former too much esteem of riches, and think them so much esteemed of by others, as that, if they seem not to the world to have them, their life is death unto them, and therefore they will be sure to make a fair outside, and appear rich, though they be nothing lesse. The other esteeming themselvs happy in having, and keeping them, conceal, and spare that theyr treasure what they can, least by haveing it known, they should be occasioned, one way, or other, to diminish it. Both are injurious to God, to other men, and

to themselvs. To God, in belying him; the former, as if he had
given them that which he hath not: the latter, as not haveing
given them that which he hath. To others, the former, in getting
into their hands the riches, which they cannot satisfy for, or credit
which they deserv not: the latter by with-holding both from
God and men their due. To themselvs, the former, in frustrateing
the occasion of humiliation, unto which the Lord by poverty
calls them: the latter, by preventing, or quenching the provoca-
tions unto thankfulness to God for his plenty bestowed upon
them, besides other comfortable effects thereof.

The Apostle poynts at some Christians (so called) that "will
be rich," even, whether God will, or no, and say he what he
will, and almost do what he can, to hinder it. They will be
rich (if it may be) keeping fayth, and good conscience in outward
profession. If that will not be, they will be rich without them;
and rayther loose their own souls then not gayn the world.
But wo be unto them; for they run greedily after the errour of
Balaam; and will have God also run with them, otherwise he
is not for their company.

6   *John Winthrop*
          A Modell of Christian Charity

*The social ideal of a community based on Christian love had a special
significance and power for the founders of New England. In establishing
a colony in the wilderness, cooperation was essential, but even more important was the feeling of the American Puritans that they had a special
commission from God. They were to build a "city upon a hill," a model
for the reformation of England and the rest of Europe. They felt that
they had to be doubly careful to restrain the tendencies in man to give*

SOURCE. John Winthrop, "A Modell of Christian Charity" (1630) from *The
Winthrop Papers*, Vol. II. Boston: The Massachusetts Historical Society, 1931,
pp. 282–284, 288–290, 292–295. Reprinted by permission of Massachusetts Historical Society.

himself to the things of this world and to forget both God and his fellow man.

As governor of the colony for most of his first twenty years, John Winthrop was the single most influential nonclerical leader in early Massachusetts. His strength of character and political skill were essential ingredients of the success of Puritanism in America. In the following selection, a lay sermon preached to the Massachusetts settlers before they landed in America, Winthrop presents the social ideal their special commission from God imposed on those who would establish a model for the reformation of the world.

A MODELL OF CHRISTIAN CHARITY

*Written
On Boarde the Arrabella,
On the Attlantick Ocean.*

By the Honorable John Winthrop Esquire.

In His passage (with the great Company of Religious people, of which Christian Tribes he was the Brave Leader and famous Governor), from the Island of Great Brittaine, to New-England in the North America.

Anno 1630

CHRISTIAN CHARITIE

A Modell Hereof.

God Almightie in his most holy and wise providence hath soe disposed of the Condicion of mankinde, as in all times some must be rich some poore, some highe and eminent in power and dignitie, others meane and in subjeccion.

The Reason Hereof.

I. REAS: First, to hold comformity with the rest of his workes, being delighted to shewe forthe the glory of his wisdome in the variety and differance of the Creatures, and the glory of his power, in ordering all these differences for the preservacion and good of the whole, and the glory of his greatness, that as it is the glory of princes to have many officers, soe this great King will have many Stewards, counting himselfe more honoured in dispenceing his gifts to man by man, then if hee did it by his owne immediate hand.

2. REAS: Secondly, That he might have the more occasion to manifest the worke of his Spirit: first, upon the wicked in moderateing and restraineing them, soe that the riche and mighty should not eate upp the poore, nor the poore and dispised rise upp against theire superiours, and shake off theire yoke; 2ly in the regenerate in exerciseing his graces in them, as in the greate ones, theire love, mercy, gentleness, temperance, etc., in the poore and inferiour sorte, theire faithe, patience, obedience etc.

3. REAS: Thirdly, That every man might have need of other, and from hence they might be all knitt more nearly together in the Bond of brotherly affeccion: from hence it appeares plainely that noe man is made more honourable then another or more wealthy etc., out of any perticuler and singuler respect to himselfe, but for the glory of his Creator and the Common good of the Creature, Man; Therefore God still reserves the propperty of these gifts to himselfe, as Ezek: 16.17.; he there calls wealthe his gold, and his silver etc.; Prov: 3.9. he claimes theire service as his due, honour the Lord with thy riches, etc. All men being thus (by divine providence) rancked into two sortes, riche and poore; under the first, are comprehended all such as are able to live comfortably by theire owne meanes duely improved, and all others are poore according to the former distribution. There are two rules whereby wee are to walke one towards another: JUSTICE and MERCY. These are allwayes distinguished in theire Act and in theire object, yet may they both concurre in the same Subject in each respect: as sometimes there may be an occasion of shewing mercy to a rich man, in some sudden danger of distresse, and allsoe of doeing of meere Justice to a poor man in regard of some perticuler contract, etc.

There is likewise a double Lawe by which wee are regulated in our conversacion, one towardes another. In both the former respects, the lawe of nature and the lawe of grace, or the morrall

lawe or the lawe of the gospell, to ommitt the rule of Justice as
not propperly belonging to this purpose otherwise then it may
fall into consideracion in some perticuler Cases. By the first of
these lawes, man as he was enabled soe withall [is] commanded
to love his neighbour as himselfe; upon this ground stands all
the precepts of the morrall lawe, which concernes our dealings
with men. To apply this to the works of mercy, this lawe requires
two things: first, that every man afford his help to another in
every want or distresse; Secondly, That hee performe this out
of the same affeccion which makes him carefull of his owne good,
according to that of our Saviour, Math: "Whatsoever ye would
that men should do to you." This was practised by Abraham
and Lott in entertaineing the Angells and the old man of Gibea.

The Lawe of Grace or the Gospell hath some differance from
the former as in these respectes: first, the lawe of nature was given
to man in the estate of innocency, this of the Gospell in the
estate of regeneracy; 2ly, the former propounds one man to
another, as the same fleshe and Image of god, this as a brother
in Christ allsoe, and in the Communion of the same spirit, and
soe teacheth us to put a difference betweene Christians and others.
Do good to all especially to the household of faith; upon this
ground the Israelites were to putt a difference betweene the
brethren of such as were strangers though not of the Canaanites.
3ly, The Lawe of nature could give noe rules for dealeing with
enemies, for all are to be considered as friends in the estate of
innocency. But the Gospell commaunds love to an enemy. Proofe:
If thine Enemie hunger feede him; Love your enemies, do good
to them that hate you, Math:5.44.

The Lawe of the Gospell propounds, likewise, a difference of
seasons and occasions; there is a time when a christian must sell
all and give to the poore as they did in the Apostles times. There
is a tyme allsoe when a christian (though they give not all yet)
must give beyone theire ability, as they of Macedonia, Cor: 2.6.
Likewise, community of perils calls for extraordinary liberallity,
and soe doth Community in some speciall service for the Churche.
Lastly, when there is noe other meanes whereby our Christian
brother may be releived in this distresse, wee must help him
beyond our ability, rather then tempt God, in putting him upon

help by miraculous or extraordinary meanes.

.   .   .   .

    Haveing allready sett forth the practise of mercy according
to the rule of gods lawe, it will be usefull to lay open the
groundes of it, allsoe being the other parte of the Commandement, and that is the affeccion from which this exercise of mercy
must arise, the Apostle tells us that this love is the fulfilling of
the lawe, not that it is enough to love our brother and soe noe
further, but in regard of the excellency of his partes giveing
any motion to the other as the Soule to the body and the power
it hath to sett all the faculties on worke in the outward exercise
of this duty, as when wee bid one make the clocke strike, he
doth not lay a hand on the hammer which is the immediate
instrument of the sound but setts on worke the first mover or
maine wheele, knoweing that will certainely produce the sound
which hee intends. Soe the way to drawe men to the workes of
mercy is not by force of Argument from the goodness or necessity
of the worke, for though this course may enforce a rationall
minde to some present Act of mercy as is frequent in experience,
yet it cannot worke such a habit in a Soule as shall make it
prompt upon all occasions to produce the same effect but by
frameing these affeccions of love in the hearte which will as
natively bring forthe the other, as any cause doth produce the
effect.

    The diffinition which the Scripture gives us of love is this:
Love is the bond of perfection. First, it is a bond, or ligament.
2ly, it makes the worke perfect. There is noe body but consistes
of partes and that which knitts these partes together gives the
body its perfection, because it makes eache parte so contiguous
to the other as thereby they do mutually participate with eache
other, both in strengthe and infirmity, in pleasure and paine; to
instance in the most perfect of all bodies, Christ and his church
make one body; the severall parties of this body considered
aparte before they were united were as disproportionate and as
much disordering as soe many contrary quallities or elements
but when Christ comes and by his spirit and love knitts all these
partes to himselfe and each to other, it is become the most perfect and best proportioned body in the world, Eph: 4.16. "Christ
by whome all the body being knitt together by every joynt for

the furniture thereof according to the effectuall power which is in the measure of every perfeccion of partes, a glorious body without spott or wrinckle, the ligaments hereof being Christ or his love, for Christ is love," I John:4.8. Soe this definition is right, Love is the bond of perfection.

From hence wee may frame these Conclusions.

I. first all true Christians are of one body in Christ. I Cor. 12.12.13.17. Ye are the body of Christ and members of parte.

2ly. The ligamentes of this body which knitt together are love.

3ly. Noe body can be perfect which wants its propper ligamentes.

4ly. All the partes of this body being thus united are made soe contiguous in a speciall relacion as they must needes partake of each others strength and infirmity, joy, and sorrowe, weale and woe. I Cor. 12:26. If one member suffers all suffer with it, if one be in honour, all rejoyce with it.

5ly. This sensibleness and Sympathy of each others Condicions will necessarily infuse into each parte a native desire and endeavour, to strengthen, defend, preserve and comfort the other.

.   .   .   .

The next consideracion is how this love comes to be wrought; Adam in his first estate was a perfect modell of mankinde in all theire generacions, and in him this love was perfected in regard of the habit, but Adam, Rent in himselfe from his Creator, rent all his posterity allsoe one from another, whence it comes that every man is borne with this principle in him, to love and seeke himselfe onely, and thus a man continueth till Christ comes and takes possession of the soule, and infuseth another principle, love to God and our brother. And this latter, haveing continuall supply from Christ, as the head and roote by which hee is united, get the predominency in the soule, soe by little and little expells the former, I John:4.7.; love cometh of god and every one that loveth is borne of god, soe that this love is the fruite of the new birthe, and none can have it but the new Creature; now when this quallity is thus formed in the souls of men, it workes like the Spirit upon the drie bones, Ezek 37., bone came to bone, it gathers together the scattered bones or perfect old man Adam and knitts them into one body againe in Christ whereby a man is become againe a liveing soule.

. . . .

From the former Consideracions ariseth these Conclusions.

I. First, This love among Christians is a reall thing, not Imaginarie.

2ly. This love is as absolutely necessary to the being of the body of Christ, as the sinewes and other ligaments of a naturall body are to the being of that body.

3ly. This love is a divine, spirituall nature, free, active, strong, Couragious, permanent, under valueing all things beneathe its propper object, and of all the graces this makes us nearer to resemble the virtues of our heavenly father.

4ly. It restes in the love and wellfare of its beloved; for the full and certain knowledge of these truthes concerning the nature, use, [and] excellency of this grace, that which the holy ghost hath left recorded, I Cor. 13., may give full satisfaccion which is needfull for every true member of this lovely body of the Lord Jesus, to worke upon theire heartes, by prayer, meditacion, continuall exercise at least of the speciall [power] of this grace till Christ be formed in them and they in him, all in eache other knitt together by this bond of love.

It rests now to make some applicacion of this discourse by the present designe which gave the occasion of writing of it. Herein are 4 things to be propounded: first, the persons, 2ly, the worke, 3ly, the end, 4ly, the meanes.

I. For the persons, we are a Company professing our selves fellow members of Christ, In which respect, onely though wee were absent from eache other many miles, and had our imploymentes as farre distant, yet wee ought to account our selves knitt together by this bond of love, and live in the exercise of it, if wee would have comforte of our being in Christ; this was notorious in the practise of the Christians in former times, as is testified of the Waldenses from the mouth of one of the adversaries, Aeneas Sylvius . . . ; they use to love any of theire owne religion even before they were acquainted with them.

2ly. for the worke wee have in hand, it is by a mutuall consent through a speciall overruleing providence, and a more than an ordinary approbation of the Churches of Christ to seeke out a place of Cohabiation and Consorteshipp under a due forme of Government, both civill and ecclesiasticall. In such cases as this the care of the publique must oversway all private respects, by which not onely conscience, but meare Civill pollicy doth bind us, for it is a true rule that perticuler estates cannott subsist in the ruine of the publique.

3ly. The end is to improve our lives, to do more service to the Lord, the comforte and encrease of the body of christe whereof we are members, that our selves and posterity may be the better preserved from the Common corrupcions of this evill world to serve the Lord and worke out our Salvacion under the power and purity of his holy Ordinances.

4ly. for the meanes whereby this must bee effected, they are 2 fold, a Conformity with the worke and end wee aime at; these we see are extraordinary; therefore wee must not content our selves with usuall ordinary meanes; whatsoever wee did or ought to have done when wee lived in England, the same must wee do and more allsoe where we goe. That which the most in theire Churches maineteine as a truthe in profession onely, wee must bring into familiar and constant practise, as in this duty of love; wee must love brotherly without dissimulation; wee must love one another with a pure hearte fervently; we must beare one anothers burdens; wee must not looke onely on our owne things, but allsoe on the things of our brethren, neither must wee think that the lord will beare with such faileings at our hands as hee dothe from those among whome wee have lived, and that for 3 Reasons.

I. In regard to the more neare bond of mariage, betweene him and us, wherein he hath taken us to be his after a most strickt and peculiar manner which will make him the more Jealous of our love and obedience, soe he tells the people of Israell, "you onely have I knowne of all the families of the Earthe therefore will I punishe you for your Transgressions."

2ly. because the Lord will be sanctified in them that come neare him. Wee know that there were many that corrupted the service of the Lord, some setting upp Alters before his owne, others offering both strange fire and strange Sacrifices allsoe; yet there came noe fire from heaven, or other sudden Judgement upon them as did upon Nadab and Abihu whoe yet wee may thinke did not sinne presumptuously.

3ly. When God gives a speciall Commission, he lookes to have it stricktly observed in every Article; when hee gave Saule a Commission to destroy Amaleck, hee indented with him upon certaine Articles, and because hee failed in one of the least, and that upon a faire pretence, it lost him the kingdome, which should have beene his reward, if hee had observed his Commission. Thus stands the cause betweene God and us: we are entered into Covenant with him for this worke; wee have taken out a Commission; the Lord hath given us leave to drawe our owne Articles; wee have professed to enterprise these Accions upon these and these ends; wee have hereupon besought him of favour and blessing. Now if the Lord shall please to heare us, and bring us in peace to the place wee desire, then hath hee ratified this Covenant and sealed our Commission, [and] will expect a strickt performance of the Articles contained in it; but if wee shall neglect the observacion of these Articles which are the ends wee have propounded, and dissembling with our God shall fall to embrace this present world and prosecute our carnall intencions, seekeing great things for our selves and our posterity, the Lord will surely breake out in wrathe against us, be revenged of such a perjured people and make us knowe the price of the breache of such a Covenant.

Now the only way to avoyde this shipwracke and to provide for our posterity is to followe the Counsell of Micah, to do Justly, to love mercy, to walke humbly with our God; for this end wee must be knitt together in this worke as one man; wee must entertaine each other in brotherly Affeccion; wee must be willing to abridge our selves of our superfluities, for the supply of others necessities; wee must uphold a familiar Commerce together in all meekeness, gentleness, patience and liberallity; wee must delight in eache other, make others Condicions our owne, rejoyce together, mourne together, labour, and suffer together, allwayes haveing before our eyes our Commission and Community in the worke, our Community as members of the same body. Soe shall wee keepe the unitie of the spirit in the bond of peace; the Lord will be our God and delight to dwell among us, as his own people, and will commaund a blessing upon us in all our wayes, soe that wee shall see much more of his widome, power, goodness, and truthe, then formerly wee have beene acquainted with. We shall finde that the God of Israel is among us, when tenn of us shall be able to resist a thousand of our enemies, when hee shall make us a prayse and glory, that men shall say of succeeding plantacions: the lord make it like that of New England. For wee must Consider that wee shall be as a Citty upon a Hill; the eyes of all people are uppon us; soe that if wee shall deale falsely with our god in this worke wee have undertaken and soe cause him to withdrawe his present help from us, wee shall be made a story and a by-word through the world; wee shall open the mouthes of enemies to speake evill of the wayes of god and all proffessours for God's sake; wee shall shame the faces of many of gods worthy servants, and cause theire prayers to be turned into Cursses upon us till wee be consumed out of the good land whether wee are goeing.

And to shutt upp this discourse with that exhortacion of Moses, that faithfull servant of the Lord, in his last farewell to Israell, Deut. 30. Belouved there is now sett before us life, and good, deathe and evill, in that wee are Commaunded this day to love the Lord our God, and to love one another, to walke in his wayes and to keepe his Commaundements and his Ordinance, and his lawes, and the Articles of our Covenant with him, that wee may live and be multiplyed, and that the Lord our God may blesse us in the land whether wee goe to possesse it: But if our heartes shall turne away soe that wee will not obey, but shall be seduced and worshipp other Gods, our pleasures, and proffitts, and serve them; it is propounded unto us this day, wee shall surely perishe out of the good Land whether wee passe over this vast Sea to possesse it;

> *Therefore lett us choose life,*
> *that wee, and our Seede,*
> *may live; by obeying his*
> *voyce, and cleaveing to him,*
> *for hee is our life, and*
> *our prosperity.*

PART THREE

Liberty Versus Reformation

7   *Edmund S. Morgan*

Roger Williams: The Church and the State

Professor Edmund S. Morgan of Yale University has produced interesting books on the era of the American Revolution and early Virginia, as well as several important works on various aspects of Puritan thought and life. Much of his writing has been biographical and all of it is highly readable.

Among the many books that have been written on Roger Williams, advocate of religious freedom and founder of Rhode Island, the most recent and in several ways the best is Morgan's Roger Williams: The Church and the State. *The implicit tension in Puritanism between the goal of an externally imposed reformation and the belief that ultimately every man must find his own salvation became explicit in the debate over religious toleration between Roger Williams and John Cotton. Morgan argues that Williams differed from the orthodox Puritans, represented by Cotton, not because his beliefs were in themselves at variance with theirs but because he held to certain common ideas with a unique consistency. In the following selections Morgan shows how this consistency led Williams to unusual attitudes toward the functions of government and liberty of conscience.*

THE INTELLECTUAL INTEGRITY OF A PURITAN HERETIC

Roger Williams lived in what he called "wonderful, searching, disputing and dissenting times." Three centuries later the description still seems accurate. From the accession of James Stuart

SOURCE. From *Roger Williams: The Church and the State,* copyright © 1967 by Edmund S. Morgan, pp. 3–5, 115–120, 137–142. Reprinted by permission of Harcourt, Brace & World, Inc., and the Author.

in 1603 to the Glorious Revolution of 1688 Englishmen thought long and hard about authority, both in church and in state, and they tried their thoughts in action. None thought longer or harder, none searched, disputed, or dissented more earnestly than Williams himself, and none was more ready to try his thoughts in action.

The facts of his life, so far as they are known, have been often and ably related: his education at Charterhouse and Cambridge, his exodus to Massachusetts in the first winter of the Puritan settlement there, his expulsion from the colony for his novel ideas, his founding of Rhode Island as a refuge for religious dissent, and his subsequent career as leader and defender of the colony and spokesman for freedom of conscience in both England and America. The history is an honorable one and has earned a place in the classic accounts of the American past. It will not be repeated here, for this is neither a biography of Williams nor a study of his colony, but an attempt to trace the way he thought.

Williams did what he did because of what he thought. Never was a man of action more an intellectual. But in the progression of his ideas we can find much more than an explanation of what he did. We can find a man thinking in an age of great intellectual expansion—not an ordinary man, for ordinary men seldom think, not a typical man, for in the end hardly anyone agreed with him, but a man nevertheless who was driven by the same intellectual forces that moved other men of that restless time. Williams was a Puritan, and in him we can watch Puritan thought exploding, hurling itself outward to its ultimate limits. The diverse internal energies that other Puritans were able to restrain and bring into uneasy harmony went unchecked in Williams. If we follow him as he allowed the force of his ideas to sweep him from the conventional to the original, from orthodoxy to heresy, we will enjoy the spectacle of a great religious imagination at work, and at the same time we will see exposed some of the hidden conflicts that tormented every Puritan.

The spectacle is not easily observed. Roger Williams' writings are voluminous, filling seven volumes in the latest edition, but they are couched in a syntax that often defies analysis: Williams could stretch a sentence to several paragraphs before bringing himself to a predicate. What is worse, for anyone interested in the way he got from one idea to another, his surviving writings, other than a few letters, were all written after his thought had reached maturity. The earliest was published in 1643, seven years after his banishment from Massachusetts. Nearly everything we know about what Williams thought before he left Massachusetts must be inferred from these later writings and from the brief and biased reports written by his opponents at the time.

A reconstruction of his intellectual development must therefore be conjectural. The conjecture may nevertheless carry a high degree of probability. Williams was a man of his time and very much a part of it. His letters reveal a warm man, outgoing and friendly, by temperament more prone to agreement than to the disagreements that his intellectual questing drove him to. The direction of his thought may thus be traced in relation to the ideas from which he started, the ideas he learned from those around him, from the masters at whose feet he sat, from the men with whom he worked and talked before he talked himself into intellectual solitude. His thinking progressed not by opposing accepted ideas, but by pursuing them through their implications to conclusions that his contemporaries could not or would not accept. The ideas with which he began are therefore visible everywhere in his mature writings, and clear signs of his most novel conclusions are already discernible in statements attributed to him during his early years in Massachusetts. From these alleged statements and from his own writings we can chart the logical, and in some measure the chronological, course of his thinking, especially his thinking about the two subjects that drew his primary attention, the church and the state. Roger Williams did write about other matters, but his treatment of them was conventional and static. The history of his ideas attempted in the succeeding pages will deal only with the way he thought about the church, the state, and the relationship between them.

THE BUSINESS OF GOVERNMENT

Government, as Williams saw it, required skills that had nothing to do with religion. Other Puritans had already recognized that rulers sometimes had to do things which would be wrong in a private man. For example, it might in some cases be good "policy" for a ruler to practice deception, as Machiavelli had counselled. It might be right for a ruler to disobey God's laws in some exceptional instance, if by doing so he could make them prevail the better among his people. By such casuistry, Puritans managed to assimilate some of Machiavelli's doctrines even while denouncing him. Williams, in repudiating the religious purposes of the state, threw over the Puritan effort to sanctify policy and recognized government more in Machiavelli's own terms as an art, like that of a pilot or of a soldier, an art with its own methods and purposes, useful to mankind, approved by God in a general way but human in origin and operation.

Christianity was not at odds with government. Indeed, Christ himself had given instructions to His followers that must make them good subjects of any government. Nor was it inconceivable that a Christian might participate in governing. Williams did not hold with those who thought that Christ had forbidden this. But he believed that, in point of fact, very few true Christians, either in the persecuted phase of Christianity before Constantine or in the apostate phase afterwards, had ever become magistrates. Christ had apparently known it would be so, for while He gave advice to His followers about their duties as subjects, He gave none about the way that Christians should conduct themselves as magistrates. Government in all ages had generally been left to men of high birth, great in wealth and wisdom, men of proven talent in the affairs of the world, and Williams never questioned the fitness of the coincidence. But since the world thus honored its own kind, and since Christ did not ordinarily honor those whom the world did, "since not many Wise and Noble are called, but the poore receive the Gospel, as God hath chosen the poore of the World to be rich in Faith," it was not to be expected that many Christians would be found among the rulers of the world.

For the same reason it was foolish to look for rulers among Christians, to require as Massachusetts did that magistrates be chosen from church members. This was to deny the state access to political talent. The Massachusetts law would thrust into government persons unfit for it and at the same time waste the abilities of others who were fit: "we know the many excellent gifts wherewith it hath pleased God to furnish many, inabling them for publike service to their Countries both in peace and War (as all Ages and Experience testifies) on whose soules hee hath not yet pleased to shine in the face of Jesus Christ: which Gifts and Talents must all lye buried in the Earth, unlesse such persons may lawfully be called and chosen to, and improved in publike service, notwithstanding their different or contrary Conscience and Worship."

In thus divorcing the ruler's calling entirely from the calling of a Christian to salvation, Williams struck at one of the springs of orthodox Puritan thinking. Puritans linked life in this world and the next by the word "calling." God called men to salvation, and He also called them to their jobs in the community where they lived. Every Puritan knew that before he undertook to be a merchant or cobbler or farmer he must have a calling from God. A minister or magistrate must likewise be called to his office. An emigrant to New England must sense a calling to come before he boarded ship. Although the voice that called might speak only through the reason or conscience, though it might be difficult to discern, and a man might be mistaken about it, he must be sure that it was the voice of God before he could be confident that he was doing right in hearkening to it. It must, in other words, be the same voice that called a Christian to salvation. Every Christian thus had two callings, usually designated as general calling and particular calling. And in performing the duties of his particular calling—in making his living and serving the community—he must always subordinate them to the duties of his general calling to serve God.

The Puritans thus joined a man's every action with his religion and laid the foundations for what a later observer was to call "worldly asceticism." Williams, in denying that the particular calling of a ruler had anything to do with the general calling of a Christian, was in effect denying that the work of this world had anything to do with Christ or Christianity. And again the observable facts seemed to bear him out: a man could be a good shoemaker or farmer, a good father or husband without being a Christian at all. And conversely "a Christian Captaine, Christian Merchant, Physitian, Lawyer, Pilot, Father, Master, and (so consequently) Magistrate, etc. is no more a Captaine, Merchant, Physitian, Lawyer, Pilot, Father, Master, Magistrate, etc. then [than] a Captaine, Marchant, etc. of any other Conscience or Religion." The members of a community might therefore go about their work honorably and successfully, whatever the state of their souls. And a community in search of a good ruler should not look simply among Christians and neglect the talents of others who were likely to be better qualified in the art of governing.

Even worse for the state than the withholding of political talent was the harnessing of government to a religious purpose. Although Williams' principal concern in the separation of church and state was to preserve the church from worldly contamination, he also believed that government suffered when diverted from its proper functions by the church. Every Protestant knew how the pope had once corrupted the governments of Europe by making them do his bidding, and Williams could count on agreement when he reminded his readers how the pope had made dogs of "the Emperours, Kings, and Magistrates of the World, whom he teacheth and forceth to crouch, to lie downe, to creepe, and kisse his foote, and from thence at his beck to flie upon such greedie Wolves, as the Waldenses, Wicklevists, Hussites, Hugonites, Lutherans, Calvinists, Protestants, Puritans, Sectaries, etc. to imprison, to whip, to banish, to hang, to head, to burne, to blow up such vile Hereticks, Apostates, Seducers, Blasphemers etc." But Williams thought that Protestants, wherever they had gained power, had done no better. Though they professed to champion the divine right of kings and governors, and even placed the government above the church, they expected the government to do what the ministers told it to do, to stamp out as heresy whatever the ministers said was heresy. And so the Protestant ministers "ride the backs and necks of Civill Magistrates, as fully and as heavily (though not so pompously)

as ever the great Whore sat the backs of Popish Princes." The assumption of religious purposes, then, was as bad for the state as
it was for the church, because it opened the way to usurpation
of civil power by the clergy, who in England, for example, had
"tost up and downe (even like Tenis-bals) the Magistrates and
Laws, the Consciences and Worships, the Peace and War, the
Weale and Woe of this Nation."

The trouble with the Puritan view as with the Catholic was
that it mistook the purpose of government. Government had
nothing to do with eternal salvation and only a tenuous connection with God at all. The purpose of government, said
Williams, was to protect the bodies and goods of its subjects.
Wherever government existed, that was the job assigned it by
the people who started it. And since government could rise no
higher than its source, it gained no further accretion of functions
or powers if the people happened to be Christian and assigned
it an authority they did not themselves possess: "that Minister or
Magistrate goes beyond his commission, who intermeddles with
that which cannot be given him in commission from the people."
Whether pagan or Christian, so long as a government protected
the people who created it, in their persons and in their property,
it did what a government ought to do. But when it tried to save
souls, it succeeded only in injuring bodies; when it tried to protect the true church, it succeeded only in transforming true
into false.

Like Machiavelli and Harrington, Williams had reached his
notion of what government ought to do by asking what government can do, not merely the government of Massachusetts or of
England but all governments. Simply to ask the question was
to cut through a mass of casuistry and confusion, created by
contending groups who saddled governments with impossible
tasks and by ambitious rulers who aspired to impossible powers.
To answer the question as Williams did—it was not the only
possible answer—was to relieve government from the pressure of
divinity and to place rulers and subjects in a new and easier
relationship with each other and with other peoples.

LIBERTY OF CONSCIENCE

Liberty of conscience meant for Williams that no man should be prevented from worshipping as his conscience directed him. It also meant that no man should be compelled to worship against his conscience or to contribute to the support of a worship his conscience disapproved. Williams did not champion liberty of conscience in religious matters because he thought conscience was any less likely to err about religion than about other things. Indeed, it was even more likely to. While many of the principles of true morality were clear even to barbarian consciences, without benefit of Scripture, the small number of Christians in the world showed how rare it was for a conscience to be right about religion. The fallibility of conscience in this respect was for most Puritans a reason for coercing it. Williams reasoned otherwise: since the men in charge of government throughout most of the world were unlikely to be Christian and unlikely to be right themselves, they would in all probability coerce conscience the wrong way, as they had ever done in the past, to the destruction of Christ's sheep.

Even in Protestant countries and among holy men, "zealous for God and his Christ," the susceptibility to error was evident everywhere. In Williams' progress from England to Massachusetts to Rhode Island he had found precious few persons whose religious consciences did not err. One need only look at the authors of the Book of Common Prayer, "in its Time, as glorious an Idoll, and as much adored by Godly persons, as any Invention now extant," yet no New Englander would have wished to have his conscience corrected by that standard. The leaders of New England had themselves gained more light after their arrival in the New World; they did not accept at the beginning some of the religious ideas that prevailed later. And who was to say that they had yet arrived at truth? What now looked like perfection in Massachusetts Bay, when viewed from heaven might "look counterfeit and ugly, and be found but (spiritually) Whores and Abominations."

How then could Puritan England or Scotland or Massachusetts suppress the testimony of those who "beleeve they see a further Light and dare not joyn with either of your Churches?" All

Protestants agreed that the Scriptures were the only source of truth about religion. Ever since the Bible had been rescued from Antichrist and restored to the people by the Reformation, it had been working a progressive enlightenment of men's consciences, revealing new and old truths to every man who searched it. But truth was not easily won, even from the Scriptures. Only by search and trial, "chewing and rational weighing and consideration" could a man arrive at a "right perswasion." If in addition to the difficulties he faced from the feebleness of his own reason, he must contend with a government that forbade him to acknowledge what he found in the Scriptures, how was either he or the government to gain more light? "In vaine have English Parliaments permitted English Bibles in the poorest English houses, and the simplest man or woman to search the Scriptures, if yet against their soules perswasion from the Scripture, they should be forced (as if they lived in Spaine or Rome it selfe without the sight of a Bible) to beleeve as the Church beleeves." England and New England needed all the light they could get from the Scriptures, and it might come from the simplest man or woman who read them as well as from the most learned minister. To prescribe one way of worship over another was to assume that the Scriptures had yielded all their truths infallibly to those who held the reins of power.

But even if a sure standard had existed by which to judge an erring conscience in religion, Williams thought it would be both wrong and useless to attempt to impose religious truth by force. The conscience, he was sure, could be corrected only by persuasion, and the application of force to it must have one of three effects, all bad: civil and corporal punishment might "cause men to play the hypocrite, and dissemble in their Religion, to turn and return with the tide, as all experience in the nations of the world doth testifie now"; it might harden the conscience in its errors, "all false Teachers and their Followers (ordinarily) contracting a Brawnie and steelie hardnesse from their sufferings for their Consciences"; or if the victim submitted and acted against his (erring) conscience, he would by so much weaken conscience itself, "since Conscience to God violated, proves (without Repentance) ever after, a very Jade, a Drug, loose and uncon-

scionable in all converse with men." Only by treating conscience
tenderly, refraining from force, could it be preserved and strengthened for the future operation of Christian persuasion and the
apprehension of God's truth.

All of Williams' ideas had a way of supporting one another,
and his view of the change wrought in history by the coming
of Christ strengthened his certainty that force must not be used
against any man's conscience in religious matters. Since the
downfall of Israel, the only true religion was that of a Saviour
who forswore the use of force. By the very attempt to coerce
conscience a magistrate demonstrated that the religion he was
enforcing was not Christian. It was "impossible for any Man or
Men to maintaine their Christ by their Sword, and to worship a
true Christ!"

But if government could do nothing with its whips and scourges
and prisons to make men Christian, Williams did not deny it all
opportunity to advance Christ's kingdom. There was one thing
government could do, though few governments had ever done it:
government could protect the free exercise of conscience in religion. Any government that properly fulfilled its obligation to
guard without discrimination the bodies and goods of all its subjects would automatically achieve this end. But it required a
vigilance and impartiality that were rare among rulers to watch
over the exercise of religion in such a way as to prevent one
group within the state from usurping authority over the consciences of other groups. When priests rode the backs of kings,
government could not fulfill this obligation. Sometimes, to be
sure, a government would throw off these tyrants of the soul and
strike a blow for freedom of conscience. Williams sang the praises
of the English Parliament for "breaking the jaws of the oppress-
ing Bishops," but he was saddened by the prospect that the same
Parliament would blemish its record "by erecting in their stead a
more refined, but yet as cruel an Episcopacy." Parliament had
failed to learn that one religious belief could be favored above
another only at the expense of truth. The Christian magistrate
could best advance the cause of his own religion by doing it no
favors.

If a civil magistrate was a Christian, he must, as an individual, submit his own soul to the spiritual government of Christ, but as a magistrate he owed the same protection to false religion as he did to his own. Williams asserted, in other words, the right of a man to be wrong about religion and to be protected in his error by the civil government. He was by no means the first Puritan to defend "liberty of conscience," but other Puritans, though admitting that a man sinned in acting against an erring conscience, were prepared to impose this sin upon him. The only liberty they allowed was a liberty to do right, and they demanded that government coerce men whose consciences led them astray, whether in morals or religion. Williams agreed as far as morals were concerned (though some of his arguments could have been applied here, he did not apply them), but in religion, the matter about which he and his contemporaries cared most, he defined liberty of conscience as the right to be wrong.

Williams' defense of liberty of conscience would seem to have been somewhat more limited than that which a Thomas Jefferson or a James Madison offered in the next century. Though Williams honored conscience in any form, he had sworn eternal warfare not against every tyranny over the mind of man but only against compulsion in religion. With a low opinion of the efficacy of human reason, his goal was not freedom of thought for its own sake: he did not think that one way of seeking God was as good as another. He wanted freedom because it was the only way to reach the true God. Although few men would reach Him at best, only freedom of conscience could bring them to Him, because Christ had foresworn the use of force. And history had demonstrated, to Williams at least, that force always favored false religion.

But the difference between Williams' view and that which ultimately prevailed in the United States is easily exaggerated. If Williams had little confidence in human reason, this fact did not separate him as far from the Founding Fathers of the United States as might at first appear. Their confidence in reason also had its limits; in framing the Constitution they tried to guard the nation against the fallibility of its own citizens. And if Williams demanded freedom of conscience because Christ demanded it, this was his way of saying what every eighteenth-

century philosopher would have applauded, that the free exercise
of reason is the only way to truth. The conscience, for Williams,
belonged to the reason, and in vindicating it he was vindicating
reason—reason corrupted by the fall of man, reason needing the
aid of Scripture and of saving grace, but reason nonetheless.

It does not follow that we should give Williams back to the
nineteenth- and twentieth-century liberals who have claimed him
for their own. Williams belonged to the seventeenth century, to
Puritanism and to Separatism. What he did share with a number
of men, in his own century as well as before and since, was a
quality that always seems to lift a man above his time: intellectual
courage, the willingness to go where the mind leads. When his
mind told him there could be no church, he left the church, even
though he wanted nothing more than to serve it. When his mind
told him the state could do nothing but harm to religion, he
said so, even though it cost him everything he had. We may
praise him (and so ourselves) for his defense of religious liberty
and the separation of church and state. He deserves the tribute
(and so perhaps do we?). But it falls short of the man. His
greatness was simpler. He dared to think.

8   Roger Williams

The Bloudy Tenent

*Roger Williams' most important work was a long, complex, and dis-
organized book written in response to a letter from John Cotton and a
plan presented by a group of New England clergy.* The Bloudy Tenent
*was published at a crucial moment in the English Civil War (1644) and
had a considerable impact on some left-wing English Puritans. Much to
the embarrassment of the Massachusetts leaders, it proved to be a very
influential book.*

SOURCE. Roger Williams, "The Bloudy Tenent of Persecution, for Cause of
Conscience . . .," 1644, from Volume III, Samuel L. Caldwell, ed., *The Complete
Writings of Roger Williams,* 1866, Perry Miller, ed. New York: Russell & Rus-
sell, 1963, pp. 1, 3, 4, 11–13, 272–273. Reprinted by permission of the publisher.

In the first of the following selections Williams presents an introductory summary of his arguments against religious persecution.

In the next selection Williams expresses his profound need to see things through to their logical conclusions, a commitment to the pursuit of truth so deep that it could even take precedence over the desire for his own salvation.

One of the fundamental differences between Williams and the orthodox Puritans was over the nature of the conscience. In the concluding selection here Williams rejects the idea that a heretic could be regarded as sinning against his own conscience. For John Cotton the conscience automatically responded to the truth once it was presented. Williams regarded the conscience as an integral part of man, a faculty that could err as well as any other. In this we can see how Williams was a genuinely modern man, modern in a way that his opponents were not. For him the integrity of the individual was more obviously real than any universal truth.

THE BLOUDY TENENT

*of Persecution, for cause of Conscience,
discussed, in A Conference betweene
TRUTH and PEACE.
Who,
In all tender Affection, present to the High
Court of Parliament, (as the Result of their
Discourse) these, (amongst other Passages)
of highest consideration.*

First, That the blood of so many hundred thousand soules of Protestants and Papists, spilt in the Wars of present and former Ages, for their respective Consciences, is not required nor accepted by Jesus Christ the Prince of Peace.

Secondly, Pregnant Scriptures and Arguments are throughout the Worke proposed against the Doctrine of persecution for cause of Conscience.

Thirdly, Satisfactorie Answers are given to Scriptures, and objections produced by Mr. Calvin, Beza, Mr. Cotton, and the Ministers of the New English Churches and others former and later, tending to prove the Doctrine of persecution for cause of Conscience.

Fourthly, The Doctrine of persecution for cause of Conscience, is proved guilty of all the blood of the Soules crying for vengeance under the Altar.

Fifthly, All Civil States with their Officers of justice in their respective constitutions and administrations are proved essentially Civill, and therefore not Judges, Governours or Defendours of the Spirituall or Christian state and Worship.

Sixtly, It is the will and command of God, that (since the coming of his Sonne the Lord Jesus) a permission of the most Paganish, Jewish, Turkish, or Antichristian consciences and worships, bee granted to all men in all Nations and Countries: and they are onely to be fought against with that Sword which is only (in Soule matters) able to conquer, to wit, the Sword of Gods Spirit, the Word of God.

Seventhly, The state of the Land of Israel, the Kings and people thereof in Peace & War, is proved figurative and ceremoniall, and no patterne nor president for any Kingdome or civill state in the world to follow.

Eightly, God requireth not an uniformity of Religion to be inacted and inforced in any civill state; which inforced uniformity (sooner or later) is the greatest occasion of civill Warre, ravishing of conscience, persecution of Christ Jesus in his servants, and of the hypocrisie and destruction of millions of souls.

Ninthly, In holding an inforced uniformity of Religion in a civill state, wee must necessarily disclaime our desires and hopes of the Jewes conversion to Christ.

Tenthly, An inforced uniformity of Religion throughout a Nation or civill state, confounds the Civill and Religious, denies the principles of Christianity and civility, and that Jesus Christ is come in the Flesh.

Eleventhly, The permission of other consciences and worships then a state professeth, only can (according to God) procure a firme and lasting peace, (good assurance being taken according to the wisedome of the civill state for uniformity of civill obedience from all sorts.)

Twelfthly, lastly, true civility and Christianity may both flour-

ish in a state or Kingdome, notwithstanding the permission of
divers and contrary consciences, either of Jew or Gentile.

THE DEMANDS OF TRUTH

While I plead the Cause of Truth and Innocencie against the
bloody Doctrine of Persecution for cause of conscience, I judge
it not unfit to give alarme to my selfe, and all men to prepare
to be persecuted or hunted for cause of conscience.

Whether thou standest charged with 10 or but 2 Talents, if
thou huntest for any cause of conscience, how canst thou say
thou followest the Lambe of God who so abhorr'd that practice?

If Paul, if Jesus Christ were present here at London, and the
question were proposed what Religion would they approve of,
The Papists, Prelatists, Presbyterians, Independents, &c. would
each say, Of mine, of mine.

But put the second question, if one of the severall sorts should
by major vote attaine the Sword of steele, what weapons doth
Christ Jesus authorize them to fight with in His cause? Do not
all men hate the persecutor, and every conscience true or false
complaine of cruelty, tyranny? &c.

Two mountaines of crying guilt lye heavie upon the backes of
All that name the name of Christ in the eyes of Jewes, Turkes
and Pagans.

First, the blasphemies of their Idolatrous inventions, superstitions, and most unchristian conversations.

Secondly, The bloody irreligious and inhumane oppressions
and destructions under the maske or vaile of the Name of
Christ, &c.

O how like is the jealous Jehovah, the consuming fire to end
these present slaughters in a greater slaughter of the holy Wit-
nesses? Rev. 11.

Six yeares preaching of so much Truth of Christ (as that
time afforded in K. Edwards dayes) kindles the flame of Q. Maries
bloody persecutions.

Who can now but expect that after so many yeares preaching
and professing of more Truth, and amongst so many great con-

tentions amongst the very best of Protestants, a firie furnace
should be heat, and who sees not now the fires kindling?

I confesse I have little hopes till those flames are over, that
this Discourse against the doctrine of persecution for cause of
conscience should passe currant (I say not amongst the Wolves
and Lions, but even amongst the Sheep of Christ themselves)
yet..., I have not hid within my breast my souls belief, And
although sleeping on the bed either of the pleasures or profits
of sinne thou thinkest thy conscience bound to smite at him
that dares to waken thee? Yet in the middest of all these civill
and spirituall Wars (I hope we shall agree in these particulars.)

First, how ever the proud (upon the advantage of an higher
earth or ground) overlooke the poore and cry out "Schismatickes,
Hereticks, &c. shall blasphemers and seducers escape unpun-
ished?" &c. Yet there is a sorer punishment in the Gospel for
despising of Christ then Moses, even when the despiser of Moses
was put to death without mercie, Heb. 10, 28, 29. He that be-
leeveth not shall bee damned, Marke 16.16.

Secondly, what ever Worship, Ministry, Ministration, the best
and purest, are practiced without faith and true perswasion that
they are the true institutions of God, they are sin, sinfull worships, Ministries, &c. And however in Civill things we may be
servants unto men, yet in Divine and Spirituall things the poorest
pesant must disdaine the service of the highest Prince: Be ye
not the servants of men, I Cor. 14.

Thirdly, without search and triall no man attaines this faith
and right perswasion, I Thes. 5. Try all things.

In vaine have English Parliaments permitted English Bibles
in the poorest English houses, and the simplest man or woman
to search the Scriptures, if yet against their soules perswasion
from the Scripture, they should be forced (as if they lived in
Spaine or Rome it selfe without the sight of a Bible) to beleeve
as the Church beleeves.

Fourthly, having tried, we must hold fast, I Thessal. 5. upon
the losse of a Crowne, Revel. 13.; we must not let goe for all
the flea bitings of the present afflictions, &c; having bought
Truth deare, we must not sell it cheape, not the least graine of
it for the whole World, no not for the saving of Soules, though

our owne most precious, least of all for the bitter sweetning of a little vanishing pleasure.

For a little puffe of credit and reputation from the changeable breath of uncertaine sons of men.

For the broken bagges of Riches on Eagles wings: For a dreame of these, any or all of these which on our deathbed vanish and leave tormenting stings behinde them: Oh how much better is it from the love of Truth, from the love of the Father of Lights, from whence it comes, from the love of the Sonne of God, who is the way and the Truth, to say as he, John 18.37., For this end was I borne, and for this end came I into the World that I might beare witnesse to the Truth.

THE INTEGRITY OF CONSCIENCE

[The New England clergy] propose a distinction of some sinnes: some are against the light of conscience, &c. and they instance in Heresie.

Ans. I have before discust this point of an Heretick sinning against light of conscience: And I shall adde that howsoever they lay this down as an infallible conclusion that all Heresie is against light of Conscience, yet (to passe by the discussion of the nature of Heresie, in which respect it may so be that even themselves may be found heretical, yea and that in fundamentalls) how do all Idolaters after light presented, and exhortations powerfully pressed, either Turkes or Pagans, Jewes or Antichristians, strongly even to the death hold fast (or rather are held fast by) their delusions.

Yea Gods people themselves, being deluded and captivated are strongly confident even against some fundamentalls, especially of worship, and yet not against the light, but according to the light or eye of a deceived conscience.

Now all these consciences walke on confidently and constantly even to the suffering of death and torments, and are more strongly confirmed in their beleefe and conscience, because such bloudy and cruell courses of persecution are used toward them.

Secondly, speakes not the Scripture expressly of the Jew, Isa. 6., Mat. 13., Acts 28., that God hath given them the spirit of slumber, eyes that they should not see, &c. all which must be spoken of the very conscience, which he that hath the golden key of David can only shut and open, and all the Picklocks or Swords in all the Smiths shops in the World can neither by force or fraud prevent his time.

Is it not said of Antichristians, 2 Thessal. 2. that God hath sent them strong delusions, so strong and efficacious, that they beleeve a Lie, and that so Confidently, and some so Conscientiously, that Death it selfe cannot part betweene the Delusion and their Conscience.

9   *John Cotton*

The Bloudy Tenent, Washed

John Cotton, Williams' great opponent, was the most famous of the New England ministers. In 1647 he replied to the Bloudy Tenent *with* The Bloudy Tenent, Washed.

Cotton was horrified by Williams' attempt to deny the religious power of the state. Without that power in the hands of the magistrate there could be no reformation. Williams had maintained that the Biblical precedent for the spiritual authority of the state which could be found in the Old Testament was not valid since the coming of Christ because it had been "typical"—that is, merely symbolic. To this Cotton reacted with shock, noting that such an argument could be used to deny all divine sanction to any kind of civil government. Cotton saw Williams as virtually atheistic, particularly since Williams' attitude toward the situation of the church in his time would have the effect of denying ecclesiastical means for rooting out heresy. For Cotton, to fail to put down false religion would be to tempt God to destroy the whole society.

In the second selection Cotton denies that he advocates the persecution of any consciences, even those that are erroneous. To him it seemed

SOURCE. John Cotton, *The Bloudy Tenent Washed*, London: 1647, pp. 66–69, 26–27.

obvious that anyone who persisted in heresy after being instructed in the truth did not follow his conscience but sinned against it. In this argument Cotton reveals the profound differences between himself and Williams regarding the nature of the conscience and the nature of man.

The structure of The Bloudy Tenent, Washed, *following that of* The Bloudy Tenent, *is disorganized. In the material that follows the discusser is Williams and the defender and the answerer represent Cotton.*

OF THE MAGISTRATES POWER

DISCUSSER: . . . "The meanes God hath appointed for preservation from spiritual infection and perdition, are spirituall. . . . But the Lord Jesus never appointed the civill sword for either Antidote, or Remedy, as an addition to those Spirituals. The Remedy which God prescribed to the Angell of the Church of Pergamus, It were a Babylonish confusion to interpret it as sent to the Governour of the City of Pergamus."

DEFENDER: . . . It is true, Christ hath appointed Spirituall means for the avoiding and preventing the infection of heresies; so hath he also for the preventing and avoiding all offences in Church-members. But that hindreth not the lawfull and necessary use of a civill sword for the punishment of some such offences, as are subject to Church-censure. If indeed the Ordinances of Christ in the Church do prevaile to the avoiding and healing of heresies, there is no need of the civill sword for that end. But it often falleth out otherwise as:

1. That when the Church hath cast out an Heretick, yet he still remaineth obstinate, and proceedeth to seduce, and destroy the faith of some, (it may be of many:) as Did Hymeneus and Philetus, 2 Tim. 3. 17.18. If the Magistrates' sword do here rust in the scabberd, such leaven may leaven the whole Masse of a City or Countrey. As by this meanes Arrianisme leavened the world by the indulgence of Constantius. . . .

2. It may be the Heretick was never any member of the Church, and then through the Church may lay in some Antidotes, and Purges, to preserve, or recover their Members, yet how shall

they succour such as are not subject to their censures? Or how shall they prevent the spreading of this noisome leprosie in private Conventicles?

"But the Lord Jesus never appointed the civill sword for an Antidote, or Remedy in such a case."

ANS: It is evident the civill sword was appointed for a remedy in this case, Deut. 13. And appointed it was, by that Angell of Gods presence, whom God promised to send with his people, as being unwilling to goe along with them himselfe, Exod. 33. 2,3. "And that Angell was Christ, whom they tempted in the wildernesse," I Cor. 10.9. And therefore it cannot truely be said that the Lord Jesus never appointed the civill sword for a remedy in such a case. For he did expressely appoint it in the Old-Testament: nor did he ever abrogate it in the New. The reason for the Law, (which is the life of the Law) is for eternall force and equity in all Ages. "Thou shalt surely kill him, because he hath fought to thrust thee away from the Lord thy God," Deut. 13.9,10. This reason is of morall, that is, of universall and perpetuall equity, to put to death any Apostate seducing Idolater, or Heretick, who seeketh to thrust away the soules of Gods people, from the Lord their God. If Magistrates be the Ministers of God in the New-Testament, (as Paul calleth them, Rom. 13,4.) And Ministers of God to execute vengence on him that doeth evill, surely either this is no evill, (to seeke to thrust away Gods people from him) or the Magistrate beareth not the sword in vaine, to execute vengeance on such an evill doer.

"Yea but such an evill, is evill onely to the inner man, not to the civill State."

ANS: But if a man imagine evill against the Lord, it is a destructive evill to a whole City, yea to a Pagan City, and God will visit such an evill with such an affliction, as shall be no lesse then utter destruction to such a City. "It shall not rise up the second time," Nabum 1.9.11.

DISCUSSER: "But the civill Magistrate hath his charge of the bodies and goods of the Subject, as the Spirituall-Officers of

Christs City or Kingdome, have the charge of their soules, and soule-safety."

DEFENDER: *Reply 1.* If it were true, that the Magistrate hath charge onely of the bodies and goods of the Subject, yet that might justly excite to watchfulnesse against such pollutions of Religion as tend to Apostacy. For if the Church and People of God fall away from God, God will visit the City and Countrey with publicke calamity, if not captivity for the Churches sake. The Idolatry and Image-worship of Christians, brought in the Turkish captivity upon the Cities and Countryes of Asia, and upon some of Europe also. . . .

Reply 2. It is a carnall and worldly, and indeed an ungodly imagination, to confine the Magistrates charge to the bodies and goods of the Subject, and to exclude them from the care of their soules. Did ever God commit the charge of the body to any Governours, to whom, he did not commit (in his way) the care of soules also? Hath God committed to Parents the charge of their childrens bodies, and not the care of their Soules? To Masters the charge of their servants bodies, and not of their soules? To Captaines the charge of their souldiers bodies and not to their soules? Shall the Captaines suffer false worship, yea idolatry, publickly professed and practised in the campe, and yet looke to prosper in the Battell?

The Magistrates to whom God hath committed the charge of bodies, and outward man of the Subject, are they not also to take care to procure faithfull Teachers to be sent amongst them? Jehosaphat tooke faithfull care for the soules of his people in this kind, 2 Chron. 17.7,8,9. Neither did he this as a Type of Christ, but as a Servant of Christ. Those things are said to be done as Types of Christ, which being ceremoniall duties, were afterwards done by Christ in his owne Person, and so were in him accomplished, and abolished, And it would be sacriledge to performe the same after him. But let the conscience of any sincere Christian judge, whether it would be sacriledge in a godly Magistrate, to procure the sending forth of godly Preachers into all the blind corners of his countrey? The truth is, Church Governours, and civill governours do herein stand paralell one to another. The Church-Governours though to them be chiefely committed the charge of soules, as their adaequate objects, yet in order to the good of the soules of their people, to dehort from idlenesse, negligence, from intemperancy in meates and drinkes, from oppression, and deceit, and therein provide both for the health' of their bodies, and the safety of their estates. So civill governours though to them be chiefely committed the bodies and goods of the people (as their ada-equate object) yet in order for this, they may, and ought to procure spirituall helpes to their soules, and to prevent such spirituall evills, as that the prosperity of Religion amongst them might advance the prosperity of the civill State.

Reply 3. I cannot but with griefe observe the sinfull guile of the Discusser, who whilest he taketh off all charges of soules from the civill Magistrates, and layeth it upon Church-Gover-nours, he taketh it off from Church-Governours, too, that so the whole charge of precious soules (for whom Christ dyed) might utterly fall to the ground. For how shall Church-Governours take the charge of soules upon them, if there be no Church Governours? And how shall there be Church-Governours where there be no Churches? If the Churches be all dissipated and rooted out from the face of the Earth by the Apostacy of Anti-christ, and none to be gathered againe, till new Apostles or Evangelists be sent abroad for such a worke, then there be now neither Churches, nor Church-Governours, nor Church-censures, either to censure Hereticks, or to fetch in those stray soules whom they have scatter'd. And then rejoyce yee Hereticks, and all yea Idolaters, and Seducers, and goe on, and make havock of the sheep of Christ like ravenous Wolves. You may now do it . . . without feare or danger; it is neither for Civill Governours, nor Church-Governours to meddle with you; Not the Civill Gover-nours, for they are not to judge nor punish in matters of Reli-gion. Nor for Church-Governours, for there are neither Churches, nor Church-Governours extant now upon the face of the Earth. But woe be to you poore sheepe and Lambes of Christ Jesus: you are now indeed truly become the "sheep of the slaughter, your Possessours may slay you, and plead themselves not guilty," (Zach. 11.4,5.) not guilty before the Civill Barre, for their crime

is exempted from civill cognizance: not guilty before the Churches
Tribunall, for there be no Churches to call them to account.

SINNING AGAINST ONE'S OWN CONSCIENCE

DISCUSSER: . . . "It is not lawful to persecute an Erroneous and
blinde Conscience, Even in Fundamentall, and weighty Points,
till after Admonition once, or twice, Tit. 3.10,11. And then such
Consciences may be persecuted, because the Word of God is so
cleare, in Fundamentall and weighty Points, that such a person
cannot but sinne against his Conscience, and so being condemned
of himselfe, that is of his Conscience, he may be persecuted for
sinning against his own Conscience."

DEFENDER: They are the words of the Discusser, not mine,
That such as erre in Fundamentall and weighty Points, after
once or twice Admonition, such Consciences are then to be
persecuted.

No, my words will cleare themselves if they be truly related,
even as himselfe hath printed them. Thus they stand.

"Secondly, For an erroneous and blinde Conscience, even in
Fundamentall and weighty Points, It is not lawfull to persecute
any, till after Admonition once or twice. And so the Apostle
directeth, Tit. 3.10. and giveth the reason, That in Fundamentall & principall Points of Doctrine and worship, the Word
of God in such things is so cleare, that he cannot but be convinced in conscience of the dangerous Error of his way, after
once or twice Admonition, wisely and faithfully dispenced. And
then, if any one persist, it is not out of Conscience, but against
his Conscience, as the Apostle saith, ver. 11. He is subverted and
sinneth being condemned of himselfe, that is, of his owne Conscience, so that if such a man after such Admonition, shall still
persist in the Error of his way, and be therefore punished, He
is not persecuted for cause of Conscience, but for sinning against
his Conscience."

Where though I say, That it is not lawfull to persecute any,
though erring in Fundamental and weighty Points, till after

once or twice admonition, I doe not therefore say, (as the Discusser reporteth me) that after once or twice admonition, then such Consciences may be persecuted, But that if such a man after such Admonition shall still persist in the Error of his way, and be therefore punished, He is not persecuted for cause of Conscience, but for sinning against his own Conscience.

OBJECT: But he that sayeth, It is not lawfull to persecute any Heretick till after once or twice admonition, He doth as much as say, that after once or twice admonition, It is then lawfull to persecute any Heretick.

ANS: Not so neither, neither every Heretick, nor in every Court. Not in every Court or Judicature, But the same Church that followed an Heretick, with once or twice admonition, was further to pursue him, if he remaine obstinate, with excommunication. My words do expresse two things:

1. That an Heretick till after once or twice admonition, may not be pursued, no nor with the Church-censure of Excommunication: but after once or twice admonition, It was then lawfull for the Church to proceed to his Excommunication.

2. My words hold forth this also, That if such an Heretick so convinced and admonished, be afterwards punished by any Censure, whether of Church or Court, It cannot be said, he is punished for his Conscience, but for sinning against his Conscience.

But it was no part of my words or meaning, to say, that every Heretick, though erring in some Fundamentall and weighty Points, and for the same excommunicated, shall forth with be punished by the Civill Magistrate, unless it do afterwards appeare, that he break forth further, either into Blasphemy, or Idolatry, or seducement of others to his Hereticall pernicious wayes.

PART FOUR

The Brotherhood of the Saints Versus the Inner Light

10   *The Boston Fathers*

The Covenant of the First Church of Boston: July 30, 1630

One of the first obligations confronting the Massachusetts settlers was the creation of churches that nominally would be branches of the Church of England but functionally Congregationalist. A small group of men settled in a particular location, all of whom recognized one another as among the saved, compacted together to worship God in accordance with Puritan beliefs. The church covenant was the written manifestation of the formation of such a congregation. It represented the collective side of Puritanism which was held in delicate balance with the individualistic tendencies implicit in the emphasis on the private examination of one's own spiritual state.

Subsequent covenants were to become more detailed, but the original covenant of the Boston Church reproduced here expresses the essential idea of Congregationalist religious brotherhood.

In the Name of our Lord Jesus Christ, & in Obedience to His holy will and Divine Ordinaunce.

Wee whose names are hereunder written, being by His most wise, & good Providence brought together into this part of

SOURCE. Arthur Blake Ellis, "The Covenant of the First Church of Boston," from *History of the First Church in Boston, 1630–1880*. Boston: Hall and Whiting, 1881, p. 3.

America in the Bay of Massachusetts, & desirous to unite our selves into one Congregation, or Church, under the Lord Jesus Christ our Head, in such sort as becometh all those whom He hath Redeemed, & Sanctifyed to himselfe, do hereby solemnly, & religiously (as in His most holy Proesence), Promisse, and bind o'selves, to walke in all our wayes according to the Rule of the Gospell, & in all sincere Conformity to His holy Ordinaunces, & in mutuall love, & respect each to other, so neere as God shall give us grace.

11   Darrett B. Rutman

Toward a New Jerusalem

Among younger historians the most outspoken critic of the approach of Perry Miller has been Darrett B. Rutman. Rejecting Miller's emphasis on the ideas expressed by Puritan intellectuals, Rutman concentrates on social and institutional history. In his major book, Winthrop's Boston, *he argues that New England's leading city actually evolved in its first two decades in a way very different from that intended by its founders.*

The following selections deal with the development of the Boston Church as a religious and social institution and the disruption produced in it by Anne Hutchinson and the Antinomian heresy.

The church organized in Boston in the summer and fall of 1630 was not the mature and elaborate church found there a decade later. Maturity and elaboration would come only with time and in response to events and changing circumstances.

SOURCE. Darrett B. Rutman, "Toward a New Jerusalem," from *Winthrop's Boston: Portrait of a Puritan Town, 1630–1649.* Chapel Hill: The University of North Carolina Press for the Institute of Early American History and Culture, 1965, pp. 98–99, 108–109, 111–112, 114–124, 126–130. Reprinted by permission of the publisher and author.

Neither was it an orthodox establishment in a milieu of Massachusetts orthodoxy. Indeed, there was initially no orthodoxy in Massachusetts Bay.

At the moment the church satisfied the general assumption that religious and moral teaching was an indispensable part of life and a necessary preparation for death. But to the early Bostonians it served as a unifying social and political organization as well as a haven for their souls, the focal point of their new environment, a bond with their neighbors, and a familiar reminder of the English parish. Similar in background, the Bostonians were still very largely strangers to each other until, within the first, small, windowless "Mud-Wall Meeting house," strangeness died. The weight of evidence indicates that the church was meant to embrace eventually all but the most reprobate; and to the extent that this goal was achieved among the original inhabitants and those coming to Boston in the years immediately following, it impressed a unity upon the population by demanding that all communicants undergo the common experience of formal admission: the confession of faith publicly given, the ceremonial offer and acceptance of the "right hand of friendship," and the acceptance of the burden of the covenant to walk in godly ways and give love and respect to all of the church. The ideal was never fact, although, as has been suggested, it approached actuality in the first years. However, even the noncommunicant attended the church, partaking of its brotherhood and guidance while excluded from its sacraments.

.   .   .   .

The coming of the ministers—particularly as their numbers and quality increased during and after 1633—effected changes in the Bay. Bringing with them those deep religious feelings which had, in the main, separated them from their conforming brethren in the English establishment, the ministers augmented the already high religious tone of the commonwealth. In old Boston Cotton had precipitated "a great *reformation. . . . Profaneness* was extinguished, *superstition* was abandoned, *religion* was embraced and practised among the *body* of the people." Now, in new Boston, he did the same. From the town and nearby communities the people crowded into his public lectures each Thursday, abandoning their work for the word of God. By October the Court of Assistants was to observe that the morning lectures were in "dyvers wayes prejudiciall to the common good" inasmuch as they brought about "the losse of a whole day" and "other charges and troubles"; henceforth, no lecture was to begin before one o'clock in the afternoon. A year later, lectures being given by the ministers were found to be "over burdensome" to both the people and the ministers, and an attempt was made to reduce their number and frequency, but to no avail.

.   .   .   .

The ministers brought with them . . . their great concern for theology and polity, their reputations for scholarship, and their pedantry. The laymen who had been directing the affairs of the commonwealth, towns, and churches turned to them increasingly for advice and counsel, particularly on matters regarding the church and morals, and the ministers, for their part, eagerly assumed the role of counselors. They were confident of their abilities in such matters. But more: Like the laymen who had ridden out to confront Elder Brown, the ministers were anxious to retain that unity which was so much a part of the medieval world—for them, only a step in the past.

There was a difference, however. The laymen has concerned themselves with outward communal unity and has sought it at times at the expense of leaving questions unresolved, considering dissension even in the interest of truth to be disruptive. In March 1634, for example, an argument broke out in the Boston lecture about the wearing of veils by women; Winthrop, "perceiving it to grow in some earnestness, interposed" and brought the discussion to an end. But to the ministers unity with regard to "fundamental and principall points" could only be established on the basis of God's pure truth, ascertained from the Bible and nature.

In England the ministers, for the most part, had been limited by the necessity of remaining true to the medieval commitment to a single and unified society and its one church; their nonconformity, pushed upon them by their desire to follow God's truth as they individually saw it and by what they considered errors propounded by the establishment, was consequently limited, for to deviate too far from the establishment was to hazard the sin-

ful pit of outright separation. When accusing Salem's Samuel
Skelton of separation in 1630, Cotton had asked, "What is more
antichristian than to set up two churches?" But New England
offered the ministers a "wide door of liberty." There was no
longer need to temporize, for truth and unity could be effected
within the new society—the ministers, like Winthrop, were uto-
pians of a sort—while casuistry would make the point that the new
society and its churches had not separated from the old. "Follow
the truth we must," Thomas Hooker was to write; and for Cotton
truth was to become "so cleare" that a dissenter could not "but
be convinced in Conscience of the dangerous Error of his way"
once it was pointed out to him. Even with regard to "thinges"
of lessre moment," where dissent "in a spirit of Christian meek-
nesse and love"—though not with "boisterous, and arrogant Spirit
to the disturbance of Civill Peace"—might be tolerated, it was
only until "god may be pleased to manifest his Trueth" to the
dissenter.

THE ANTINOMIAN CONTROVERSY AND ITS EFFECTS
ON THE BOSTON CHURCH

It was in Boston . . . that both dissent among the ministers
and popular enthusiasm reached their highest peak. The first
was presaged early in 1636 when the Reverend Thomas Shepard,
having attended Cotton's Thursday lecture, returned home to
Newtown in consternation. Cotton had spoken of faith and
sanctification in terms which seemed to contradict Shepard's
teachings, and Shepard wrote to ask a series of questions: "It is
the earnest desire not only of my selfe, but of diverse of our
members, whose harts are much endeared to you, that for the
further clearing up of the truth, you would be pleased to give us
Satisfaction by way of writing rather than by speech for this one
time to these particulars. . . . I have plainly writ my hart unto
you, being preswaded that in the spirit of meekness, you will not
thinke I have thus writ to begin or breed a quarrell; but to still
and quiet those which are secretly begun." Cotton had responded
in kind: "As for difference, and Jarres, it is my unfeigned desire

to avoide them with all men especially with Brethren; but I doe not know, I assure you, any difference, much less Jarres between me, and any of my Brethren in our Publique Ministery." Yet he was in error. There was a fundamental difference.

To such as Shepard, the holy church of Christ as an institution among men was all important, and feeling that sanctification—the moral behavior of the individual—was the principal sign by which man and the churches could hope to recognize God's elect, they were content to build their churches upon visible morality, calling their listeners to a reformation of their lives and inviting those of moral appearance to apply for church membership. True, the reprobate could not be transformed into a saint, nor could a man profit by his good works, storing up credits in heaven which would be counted in his favor at the Judgment, for those whom God would save were already known to Him. But the saint, living in sin, could be awakened (if it were God's will) to follow his duty toward God, while a man who could look upon his total life and say "I have lived as God would have me live according to His revealed word" could take comfort in the possibility that he was of the elect, for God's saints (by virtue of their election) would abide by God's commandments and ally themselves with the true church.

Cotton, concerned more with the individual than the institution, more with salvation than morality, would go further. He had earlier introduced the idea that admission to the church should be dependent not merely on the outward behavior and knowledge of the faith of the applicant, but on the church's evaluation of the applicant's profession of the working of Christ within him—a subtle but profound change in the admission procedure, in time transforming the church from a gathering of the professedly godly to a gathering of the professed visible saints. Other churches in Massachusetts were adopting the profession of grace as part of the admissions procedure, the would-be members being required to acknowledge "the great mercy and grace of God, in receiving them to his grace: and changing their heart and life by such or such means." But in most it remained secondary to the formal confession of knowledge of the faith and the evidence of good conduct; that the profession of grace was

"weakly" and "briefly done . . . mindes not," a 1637 statement
of admission procedures stipulated.

For Cotton, however, the profession of grace was cardinal. It
was not enough, however. Like any other minister he sought to
join men to the church, urging them to accept (and declare to
the congregation) what they felt to be God's help in renouncing
their sins and embarking upon a reformed life. The number of
conversions in the years immediately after his arrival indicates
a great response to his appeal. But membership in the church
was only an outward indication or, as he termed it, a "seal" of
the individual's saved condition, and a slight one at that. Cotton
sought to move his communicants into a pitiless self-examination,
a never-ending search for a second and true seal, driving his
words into the very entrails of his hearers. "It is the desire of
my heart by the grace of Christ," he wrote, "to provoke Christians
(in this countrye of universal professein) not to rest in any
changes of graces, Deutyes or Ordinances (as Church-fellowship
etc.) ." "I would not wish christians to build the signes of their
Adoption [by Christ] upon any sanctification, but such as floweth
from faith in Christ Jesus; for all other holynesse, and righteous-
nes . . . may be . . . mortall seede, and fall short of perseverance:
whereas the least seede of fayth, and of that holynes which floweth
from it abideth for ever." Take comfort in the true ordinances
of the church, but "while you enjoy them, trust not in them,
nor thinke not to stand upon this. that you are blessed in regard
of them." Take comfort, too, in the Word and in following its
commandments, but do not let it close your eyes to the nearness
of God Himself, "for it is not all the *promises* in Scripture, that
have at any time wrought any gracious changes in any soul, or
are able to beget the faith of *God's Elect*." Only true faith–faith
emanating directly from God, faith in the absolute perfection
of God's will and the utter desirability of "closing" with God,
faith that leads one to say "here am I as you have created me,
weak, abject, yearning for your comfort yet comforted only as it
befits your will"—only such faith is "the Witnesse of the Spirit
it selfe, as it is distinguished from our Spirit." And it was such a
witness of the holy spirit within for which he would have his
hearers search. "God giveth us his sonne and his Spirit in a
promise of grace, when he giveth Faith to the soule," he wrote;

it infuses with a perfect and irrevocable promise of salvation, and all other signs of justification, while encouraging to the individual, should not assure him of God's intention.

As abstract theology, Cotton's doctrine was not dangerous. But transferred through his teaching to the public mind there was danger indeed, and this was what worried Shepard. To stress to such an extent the personal quest for evidence of God's grace, to dismiss the ordinances of the church as comforting but ineffectual, to preach God's spirit rather than the moral law, absolute faith rather than conduct, was to unleash an individual approach to God undermining all formal religion.

This was what Cotton was doing in Boston, first among those who had followed him from old Boston to new—the Leveretts, Haughs, Hibbenses, Heatons, Hutchinsons, Coddingtons, Quincys —then spreading through the town. Anne Hutchinson, who had followed her beloved teacher to the New World, was a logical vehicle for translating the teacher's doctrine into language which the everyday townspeople could understand. Of brilliant mind and rapier-like wit, educated far above the average woman of the time, Anne began explaining and elaborating upon Sabbath and lecture-day sermons for the other women of the town shortly after her arrival in 1634. In the enthusiasm of the time her meetings were considered only a "profitable and sober carriage of matters" and a fit expression of the injunction in Titus "that the elder women should instruct the younger." But by 1636 her meetings included both men and women, and Anne was holding forth twice a week to between sixty and eighty persons. Her intellectual fare was drawn from Cotton's discourses, though the master's words gained something in the retelling: "The person of the Holy Ghost dwells" in the elect; "no sanctification can help to evidence to us" our own election, only the knowledge of the spirit within; without the union of spirit and flesh, one "remains dead to every spiritual action, and hath no gifts of graces," the pretences of such being mere hypocrisy.

By October Mrs. Hutchinson's activities had come to the attention of the other ministers of the Bay, and they appeared in Boston to investigate and, "if need were," remonstrate with the Boston church about them. But it was too late. In the rarified religious atmosphere Anne's views had swept up the greater part of the church and town, from Harry Vane, "a young gentleman of excellent parts" who had eschewed preferment at the court of Charles II to savor "the power of religion," to William Dinely, the barber-surgeon. Vane, arriving late in 1635 and well regarded for his high birth, had been elected governor in May 1636 and had carried Anne's views into the council chamber. Dinely dispensed them in a more plebeian way: "So soone as any were set downe in his chaire," wrote the orthodox Edward Johnson later, "he would commonly be cutting of their haire and the truth together." To such as these, the ministers—including Wilson but excluding Cotton and the Reverend John Wheelwright, Anne's brother-in-law and a new arrival to the commonwealth—were among those with "no gifts or graces." Without the spirit themselves, they could not preach the spirit to their hearers; hence they were but "legal teachers," drawing their congregations to hypocrisy by holding out obedience to the moral law as the way to salvation. Less than a week after the ministers met in Boston the Hutchinson faction was openly working to have Wheelwright called to be a third minister in the Boston church.

Wheelwright's bid for office in the First Church was blocked on the basis that he was desired by those who sought to gather a church at Braintree. But this was not the end of the dissension. The debate over Wheelwright thrust the Hutchinsonian opinions and their origins in Cotton's teachings into the limelight, precipitating almost two years of confused, chaotic conflict involving Boston and the whole commonwealth. The terminology of the argument was theological, and all sides displayed the exuberant righteousness which only a theological dispute among persons convinced that heaven and hell await the results can have. Yet at stake were the community itself, Winthrop's "Citty upon a Hill," and the ministers' godly truth.

Anne Hutchinson was disruption personified. Where Winthrop would find his way to God by living a godly, useful life in an orderly society committed to God, the Hutchinsonians found their way by direct and personal revelations. They divided men into believers and non-believers, saints and damned, and took themselves alone for saints. Ministerial authority was denounced

as men of Wilson's and Shepard's and Peter's caliber were casti-
gated as false teachers, undeserving of even polite attention.
They walked out when Wilson rose to speak, or, if they stayed,
heckled him with comments and questions; not content, they
streamed out of the town to public lectures elsewhere, heckling
and questioning again, badgering all whose doctrines disagreed
with theirs. They followed Cotton, but twisted his words. When
he spoke of sanctification being a natural concomitant of election
but not a sign of it, they heard (and repeated) only his denunciation; when he spoke of faith and spirit they heard only spirit
and declared faith to be as erroneous a ground for assurance of
election as sanctification. Indeed, they dismissed Cotton, however
inadvertently, by their anti-intellectualism, for by pronouncing
the personal discovery of the Holy Ghost within as the only
"infallible certaine evidence of our Justifyed [or elect] estate"
they effectively discarded the church (and Cotton) as mediator
between themselves and God. For them, truth was a lightning
flash in the night sky, illuminating God's world to the elect, not
a painful searching out of Scripture. To one Hutchinsonian,
Anne was "a Woman that Preaches better Gospell then any of
your black-coates that have been at the Ninneversity." "For my
part, saith hee, I had rather hear such a one that speakes from
the meere motion of the spirit, without any study at all, then
any of your learned Scollers, although they may be fuller of
Scripture."

Church, state, all the orderly processes of society were required
to bow before the revealed truth of the Hutchinsonians. "When
enymies to the truth oppose the way of God," John Wheelwright
told the Bostonians in a fast-day sermon early in 1637, "we must
lay loade upon them, we must kille them with the worde of the
Lorde." And if this were to "cause a combustean in Church and
Commonwealth," then so it must, for "did not Ch[rist] come to
sende fier upon the earth?" The sermon frightened the Win-
throps and Wilsons of the Bay, for they remembered the bloody
swath such enthusiasm had cut in Germany. Wheelwright was
tried by the General Court and found guilty of sedition. But
the Hutchinsonians would not rest. A remonstrance in Wheelwright's favor was prepared and distributed. Winthrop sought

to curb it: "You invite the bodye of the people, to joyn with you in your seditious attempt against the Court, and the Authority here established against the rule of the Apostel, who requires every soule to be subject to the higher powers and every Christian man, to studye to be quiet, and to meddle with his own business." Anne herself best expressed the challenge to authority. "You have power over my body but the Lord Jesus hath power over my body and soul," she told her judges when brought to trial in 1637: "If you go on in this course you begin you will bring a curse upon you and your posterity, and the mouth of the Lord hath spoken it."

Such views provoked the wrath of the commonwealth. "Antinomian," "Familist," "Erronist," "this red Regiment"—so the Hutchinsonians were termed as magistrates and ministers alike moved to break their hold on Boston. It was traumatic. "Your complaynt of the want of Brotherly love, I needes say is too just," a friend wrote Cotton in March 1637; "I [have] found soe much Strangeness, alienation, and soe much neglact from some whoe would sometimes have visited me with diverse myles going (yett here, will passe by my dore, as if I were the man that they had not knowen)." And Margaret Winthrop, writing to her husband John: "Sad thoughts possess my spirits, and I cannot repulse them, which makes me unfit for anything, wondering what the Lord means by all these troubles among us." But it was easily done, for despite the appearances of strength the Hutchinsonians did not form a strong party. They were but a mob scrambling after God, and like all mobs, quickly dispersed once their leaders were dealt with.

Vane was excluded from the government in a tumultuous election in May 1637, and sailed for England in the late summer, his reputation on both sides of the Atlantic temporarily darkened. By a series of astute maneuvers Bostons political leaders—almost to a man committed to the Hutchinsonians—were, if not silenced, rendered ineffectual. Cotton, whose views, "too obscurely" stated, continued to be used to support their position as the conflict raged in 1637, was weaned away in a succession of conferences with his fellow ministers and the commonwealth's lay leaders. The conferees did not change his views, but they brought him to see the extreme position of those who claimed him for their master and the shattering effects of their doctrines on the churches, the ministry, and the state. With Cotton neutralized, the ministers met in synod in August to catalogue and denounce the Hutchinsonian errors. All the while the First Church was being barraged with lectures and sermons, John Davenport, for example, expounding on "the nature and danger of divisions, and disorders." Finally, the more vocal Hutchinsonians were brought to trial before the General Court. Their conviction in November was assured, for the commonwealth leaders had already agreed "that two so opposite parties could not contain in the same body" and determined "to send away some of the principal." Anne herself was convicted of "traduceing mi[niste]rs and their ministery in this country" and committed to custody until the Court should enforce an order banishing her. Wheelwright, his sentencing postponed since March, was ordered to leave the commonwealth within fourteen days. Others were penalized, the list spanning Boston's social spectrum and including two deputies, three selectmen, and a deacon of the church: John Coggshall, disfranchised and "enjoyned not to speake any thing to disturbe the publike peace, upon pain of banishment"; William Aspinwall, disfranchised and banished; William Baulston, disfranchised, barred from public office, and fined twenty pounds; Edward Hutchinson, disfranchised, ousted from office, fined forty pounds, and committed "dureing the pleasure of the Courte"; Richard Gridley, disfranchised; William Dinely, disfranchised; John Underhill, disfranchised and ousted from his militia captaincy. Ten others, threatened with the same penalties, signified their submission by denouncing their part in the Wheelwright remonstrance.

The humbling of Boston followed. Fifty-eight of the townsmen were required to give up their arms and ammunition, not to receive them back again until they "acknowledg their sinn in subscribing the seditious libell" contained in the remonstrance. It was a demand for a symbolic and conscious surrender and the Bostonians knew it. But while the order "troubled some of them very much," as Winthrop wrote, "especially because they were to bring them in themselves," they meekly obeyed. A few tried to continue the struggle within the church, attempting to have the Governor called to account before the congregation for his actions during Anne's trial. The effort was easily turned aside.

By ones and twos, then in groups, the Bostonians appeared before the magistrates to acknowledge their previous errors. Those who would not recant—William Coddington and his family, for example—left. More than twenty families followed Wheelwright north beyond the Merrimac River; an equal number traveled south to Narragansett Bay, first to attempt an absolute theocracy, then to split into voluble, argumentative sects. In March 1638 Boston's humiliation was completed as Anne, for "divers Errors. and unsound Opinions," was brought before the people she had once moved so deeply to be dealt with "in a church way." Cotton, Wilson, Shepard, Eliot, Welde, Peter, Davenport—all the leading ministers of the Bay were there to go through the formality of attempting to bring her to see the truth of God. For some in the congregation it was too much: Thomas Savage, Edward Gibbons, and one of Anne's sons. But it was a sporadic, divided opposition, easily overborne by the assembled ministers. At one interruption Wilson shouted, "Should one mans scruple or doubt hinder all the rest of the Congregation, which are satisfied, to crye out, that the Lord is God, the Lord is God, and the Lord only is the Lord?" In the end Anne was excommunicated, the majestic but horrible phrases rolling from Pastor Wilson: "In the name of our Lord Jes[us] Ch[rist] and in the name of the Church . . . *I doe cast yow out . . . I doe deliver you up to Sathan* . . . I doe account yow from this time forth to be Hethen and a Publican. . . . *I command yow* in the name of Ch[rist] Je[sus] and of this Church *as a Leper to wthdraw your selfe.*"

Religious enthusiasm had given rise to the disturbances of 1637 and 1638; a statement of religious orthodoxy was to emerge from it as the ministers combined to declare truth and the magistrates sought to uphold it. Yet orthodoxy in Massachusetts was to be a curious thing. It involved no great statement of creed or belief. Truth in such matters was defined in negative terms by virtue of the condemnation of Anne's multitude of errors: Thou shalt not believe "that those . . . that are united to Ch[rist] have 2 Bodies, . . . [Christ's] and a new Body"; "That the first Thinge we

receave for our Assurance is our Election," that revelations "are
to be beleeved as well as Scripture because the same holy Ghost
did indite both." But what one should believe as credo was left
unstated.

.   .   .   .

Boston's First Church and its teacher, as they emerged from
the dissensions of the 1630's, reflected this orthodoxy. Teacher
Cotton still provoked men to go beyond outward morality and
search their souls for the spirit of God; but more and more, in
writings dealing with the nature of God's church, he was a
spokesman for orthodoxy. Within the church itself, the officers
assumed precedence, sitting apart from the congregation on
raised benches, meeting privately as the presbytery to prepare
what was in effect an agenda for the church. The process had
begun earlier. During the controversy over Roger Williams, the
officers had considered and answered a letter from the Salem
church without referring it to the congregation, brushing aside
Salem's complaint that it was only the prelatical who considered
the people "weak . . . giddy and rash" and hence incapable of
dealing with such matters. But by 1640 the power which Winthrop had earlier ascribed to the congregation was formally
redefined by the ministers as: "Libertie to enter into the fellowship of [the] church . . . to chose and call well gifted men to
office . . . to partake in sacraments . . . to joyn with officers in
the due censure of offenders and the like." Real authority was
in theory vested only in the assembled elders. "The Gospel
alloweth no Church authority (or rule properly so called) to the
Brethren, but reserveth that wholly to the Elders," Cotton wrote
in 1644.

It was emerging orthodoxy which Thomas Lechford saw in
Boston during a sojourn in the town at the turn of the decade and
which he described on his return to England. Morning and
afternoon on a Sabbath (at nine and two) the people gathered
in the meetinghouse to the tolling of the town bell. Pastor Wilson
standing "above all people in a pulpit of wood, and the Elders
on both sides," opened the morning service with a "solemn
prayer" of a quarter-hour or more, followed by Teacher Cotton
reading and expounding upon a chapter of Scripture, then a

psalm, the congregation singing unaccompanied as the ruling
elders lined out the words for them to follow:

The Lord to mee a shepheard is,
want therefore shall not I.
Hee in the folds of tender-grasse,
doth cause mee downe to lie.

In the stillness following the last phrases of the tune the pastor
rose again to begin the sermon. Sometimes Wilson would add an
exhortation based on recent happenings in the town; sometimes
he would call on a visiting minister to speak. A final prayer by
the teacher, a blessing, and the congregation filed out. Once a
month, however, the morning session was extended as the Lord's
Super was celebrated. The non-members having withdrawn, a
table was brought to the center of the meeting and the ministers
and ruling elders took seats around it; the bread was broken and
laid on a "charger" and the wine poured into a chalice, Cotton
and Wilson alternating the service. As the people watched—
standing on their seats and crowding the aisle—first the bread,
then the wine were consecrated and passed around the table to
the seated elders. Later they were circulated by the deacons to
the people as one of the ministers droned on in prayer. A psalm,
joyous,

O Give thee thanks unto the Lord,
because that good is hee

and a blessing ended the service.

In the afternoon the meetinghouse was filled again. The
worship was shorter, an opening prayer, a psalm, and Cotton's
sermon. But the meeting ran on into the evening, for the business
of the church had to be taken care of. Baptisms followed the
sermon, the pastor or teacher descending from the elders' bench
to stand by the deacons' seat, "the most eminent place in the
church, next under the Elders," as a single parent, a member of
the church, carried the child up to be sprinkled "into the name
of the *Father,* and of the *Sonne,* and of the *holy Ghost.*" As the
minister finished, one of the three deacons rose: "Brethren of
the congregation, now there is time left for contribution, wherefore as God hath prospered you, so freely offer." Pastor and

teacher at times pressed "a liberall contribution, with effectuall exhortations out of Scripture," and the people—"Magistrates and chiefe Gentlemen first" and including "most of them that are not of the church"—filed down the aisle to bring their offerings to the deacons' seat, putting money into a wooden box set out for the purpose, or, if they brought goods, laying them down before the deacons. The admission of new members and the disciplining of those who had slid from righteousness, together with the resolution of various church problems followed and continued on until dusk, the ruling elders propounding the questions and leading whatever discussion there might be (for it was they who *"open the doors of speech and silence* in the assembly"), the members signifying their consent by their silence. If time allowed—and in winter, after shivering through hours in the unheated meetinghouse, there was seldom time—the congregation joined in a final psalm, Pastor Wilson prayed, and the meeting broke up with a final blessing on all.

The "inconsequentials" of the services might vary from church to church, but the proceedings invariably reflected the transformation which was taking place. From being the font of church power, the communicants were coming to be viewed as but silent partners to their officers. "Elders be in a superior order, by reason of their office," Cotton declared; "the brethren (over whome the Elders are made Overseers and Rulers) they stand also in an order, even in orderly subjection, according to the order of the Gospel." Christ himself had ordained the structure of the church, designating its parts and duties: The *"Elders who Labour in the Word and Doctrine"* to preach *"of the word with all Authoritie"* and offer the sacraments in God's name; ministerial and lay elders to administer the affairs of the church "with an audible and lively voyce, in the open face of the Brethren of the Congregation"; the deacons to collect and dispense the funds of the church and to attend on the ministers, "wayting" on them "as their servant." The role of the members was to "readily yeeld obedience to their Overseers, in whatsoever they see and hear by them commanded to them from the Lord," for while they choose their officers, "the office itself is ordained immediately by Christ, and the rule annexed to the office, is limited by Christ only."

Cotton used a metaphor drawn from the sea to explain the relationship between the congregation and its officers: "A Queene may call her servants, her mariners, to pilot and conduct her over the Sea to such an Haven: yet they being called by her . . . shee must not rule them in steering their course, but must submit herselfe to be ruled by them, till they have brought her to her desired Haven. So is the case between the Church and her Elders."

The queen should not question the crew. Hence the questioning of points of doctrine so rampant in the Hutchinsonian outburst was considered, if not unlawful, then unnecessary. The decisions of the crew, though presented to the queen, were to be consented to by her without hesitation. Hence, questions of church administration—including admissions and discipline—were presented to the communicants. But the elders had already pondered and decided the questions. The would-be member applied first to the presbytery, made his confessions of faith and of the workings of grace within him before the assembled officers, and was subjected to their scrutiny; the member feeling aggrieved by another brought his grievance before the elders, who considered "whether the offence be really given or no, whether duely proved, and orderly proceeded in," and who had the authority to dismiss "causelesse and disorderly" charges or "propound and handle just complaints." The application for membership or the grievances were presented a second time to the whole church—though it should be noted that in the case of women applying for membership Cotton had his way and their confessions were merely read in the open meeting. But consulting the congregation was to all intents and purposes a mere formality, the elders declaring "what the *Law* . . . of *Christies*" might be, and the church of necessity concurring. Indeed, there could in theory be no dispute among the saints. The truth of God on any question, once pointed out, was instantly recognizable to those to whom Christ had promised "godly concord and agreement" and "his owne gracious presence." Dissent might arise, but it would emerge from the "corruptions and distempers of men," and if by argument the dissenters would not yield, they could be admonished for their error (as those dissenting to the excommunication of Anne Hutchinson had been) and, standing under censure, their voices would not count. The will of God, found in the Word and expounded by the elders, would be unanimously affirmed.

PART FIVE

Chosenness Versus Universality

12

Perry Miller

Errand Into the Wilderness

The Puritans had a profound sense of the importance of their venture into the New World. They saw themselves as a covenanted people, chosen by God to establish a model of universal reformation. Their mission was by no means for themselves alone.

Yet there was an implicit tension between their conception of themselves as a specially covenanted people and the responsibility for mankind that their covenant implied. To the extent that they could see themselves as acting with the world's eyes on them it was possible for them to maintain the feeling that they had been chosen to serve others, that they were a special people only instrumentally. As they ceased to be a major center of European attention, it became increasingly harder for them to maintain the balance between their sense of destiny and their universal purpose. Pride in their chosenness gradually came to overshadow the consciousness of the purpose for which they had been chosen.

The following essay by Perry Miller is a gem of condensation and implication, one of the greatest short pieces in all American historiography. As Miller suggests, the dual errand of the Puritans has had profound effects on the subsequent development of American ideas and attitudes.

SOURCE. Reprinted by permission of the publishers from Perry Miller, *Errand Into the Wilderness*, pp. 1–15, Cambridge, Massachusetts: The Belknap Press of Harvard University Press. Copyright 1956 by the President and Fellows of Harvard College.

It was a happy inspiration that led the staff of the John Carter Brown Library to choose as the title of its New England exhibition of 1952 a phrase from Samuel Danforth's election sermon, delivered on May 11, 1670: *A Brief Recognition of New England's Errand into the Wilderness.* It was of course an inspiration, if not of genius at least of talent, for Danforth to invent his title in the first place. But all the election sermons of this period— that is to say, the major expressions of the second generation, which, delivered on these forensic occasions, were in the fullest sense community expression—have interesting titles; a mere listing tells the story of what was happening to the minds and emotions of the New England people: John Higginson's *The Cause of God and His People in New-England* in 1663, William Stoughton's *New England's True Interest, Not to Lie* in 1668, Thomas Shepard's *Eye-Salve* in 1672, Urian Oakes's *New England Pleaded With* in 1673, and, climactically and most explicitly, Increase Mather's *A Discourse Concerning the Danger of Apostasy* in 1677.

All of these show by their title pages alone—and, as those who have looked into them know, infinitely more by their contents— a deep disquietude. They are troubled utterances, worried, fearful. Something has gone wrong. As in 1662 Wigglesworth already was saying in verse, God has a controversy with New England; He has cause to be angry and to punish it because of its innumerable defections. They say, unanimously, that New England was sent on an errand, and that it has failed.

To our ears these lamentations of the second generation sound strange indeed. We think of the founders as heroic men—of the towering stature of Bradford, Winthrop, and Thomas Hooker— who braved the ocean and the wilderness, who conquered both, and left to their children a goodly heritage. Why then this whimpering?

Some historians suggest that the second and third generations suffered a failure of nerve; they weren't the men their fathers had been, and they knew it. Where the founders could range over the vast body of theology and ecclesiastical polity and produce profound works like the treatises of John Cotton or the subtle psychological analyses of Hooker, or even such a gusty though wrongheaded book as Nathaniel Ward's *Simple Cobler,* let alone such lofty and rightheaded pleas as Roger Williams' *Bloudy Tenent,* all these children could do was tell each other that they were on probation and that their chances of making good did not seem very promising.

Since Puritan intellectuals were thoroughly grounded in grammar and rhetoric, we may be certain that Danforth was fully aware of the ambiguity concealed in his word "errand." It already had taken on the double meaning which it still carries with us. Originally, as the word first took form in English, it meant exclusively a short journey on which an inferior is sent to convey a message or to perform a service for his superior. In that sense we today speak of an "errand boy"; or the husband says that while in town on his lunch hour, he must run an errand for his wife. But by the end of the Middle Ages, errand developed another connotation: it came to mean the actual business on which the actor goes, the purpose itself, the conscious intention in his mind. In this signification, the runner of the errand is working for himself, is his own boss; the wife, while the husband is away at the office, runs her own errands. Now in the 1660's the problem was this: which had New England originally been— an errand boy or a doer of errands? In which sense had it failed? Had it been despatched for a further purpose, or was it an end in itself? Or had it fallen short not only in one or the other, but in both of the meanings? If so, it was indeed a tragedy, in the primitive sense of a fall from a mighty designation.

If the children were in grave doubt about which had been the original errand—if, in fact, those of the founders who lived into the later period and who might have set their progeny to rights found themselves wondering and confused—there is little chance of our answering clearly. Of course, there is no problem about Plymouth Colony. That is the charm about Plymouth: its clarity. The Pilgrims, as we have learned to call them, were reluctant voyagers; they had never wanted to leave England, but had been obliged to depart because the authorities made life impossible for Separatists. They could, naturally, have stayed at home had they given up being Separatists, but that idea simply did not occur to them. Yet they did not go to Holland as though on an errand; neither can we extract the notion of a mission out of the reasons which, as Bradford tells us, persuaded them to leave Leyden for "Virginia." The war with Spain was about to be resumed, and the economic threat was ominous; their migration was not so much an errand as a shrewd forecast, a plan to get out while the getting was good, lest, should they stay, they would be "intrapped or surrounded by their enemies, so as they should neither be able to fight nor flie." True, once the decision was taken, they congratulated themselves that they might become a means for propagating the gospel in remote parts of the world, and thus of serving as steppingstones to others in the performance of this great work; nevertheless, the substance of their decision was that they "thought it better to dislodge betimes to some place of better advantage and less danger, if any such could be found." The great hymn that Bradford, looking back in his old age, chanted about the landfall is one of the greatest passages, if not the very greatest, in all New England's literature; yet it does not resound with the sense of a mission accomplished—instead, it vibrates with the sorrow and exultation of suffering, the sheer endurance, the pain and the anguish, with the somberness of death faced unflinchingly:

"May not and ought not the children of these fathers rightly say: Our fathers were Englishmen which came over this great ocean, and were ready to perish in this wilderness; but they cried unto the Lord, and he heard their voyce, and looked on their adversitie. . . ."

We are bound, I think, to see in Bradford's account the prototype of the vast majority of subsequent immigrants—of those Oscar Handlin calls "The Uprooted": they came for better advantage and for less danger, and to give their posterity the opportunity of success.

The Great Migration of 1630 is an entirely other story. True, among the reasons John Winthrop drew up in 1629 to persuade himself and his colleagues that they should commit themselves to the enterprise, the economic motive frankly figures. Wise men thought that England was over-populated and that the poor would have a better chance in the new land. But Massachusetts Bay was not just an organization of immigrants seeking advantage and opportunity. It had a positive sense of mission—either it was sent

on an errand or it had its own intention, but in either case the
deed was deliberate. It was an act of will, perhaps of willfulness.
These Puritans were not driven out of England (thousands of
their fellows stayed and fought the Cavaliers)—they went of their
own accord.

So, concerning them, we ask the question, why? If we are not
altogether clear about precisely how we should phrase the answer,
this is not because they themselves were reticent. They spoke as
fully as they knew how, and none more magnificently or cogently
than John Winthrop in the midst of the passage itself, when he
delivered a lay sermon aboard the flagship *Arabella* and called it
"A Modell of Christian Charity." It distinguishes the motives of
this great enterprise from those of Bradford's forlorn retreat, and
especially from those of the masses who later have come in quest
of advancement. Hence, for the student of New England and of
America, it is a fact demanding incessant brooding that John
Winthrop selected as the "doctrine" of his discourse, and so as
the basic proposition to which, it then seemed to him, the errand
was committed, the thesis that God had disposed mankind in
a hierarchy of social classes, so that "in all times some must be
rich, some poor, some highe and eminent in power and dignitie;
others mean and in subjeccion." It is as though, preternaturally
sensing what the promise of America might come to signify for
the rank and file, Winthrop took the precaution to drive out of
their heads any notion that in the wilderness the poor and the
mean were ever so to improve themselves as to mount above
the rich or the eminent in dignity. Were there any who had
signed up under the mistaken impression that such was the
purpose of their errand, Winthrop told them that, although
other peoples, lesser breeds, might come for wealth or pelf, this
migration was specifically dedicated to an avowed end that had
nothing to do with incomes. We have entered into an explicit
covenant with God, "we haue professed to enterprise these
Accions vpon these and these ends"; we have drawn up indentures
with the Almighty, wherefore if we succeed and do not let ourselves get diverted into making money, He will reward us.
Whereas if we fail, if we "fall to embrace this present world and
prosecute our carnall intencions, seeking great things for our

selves and our posterity, the Lord wil surely breake out in wrathe against us be revenged of such a perjured people and make us knowe the price of the breache of such a Covenant."

Well, what terms were agreed upon in this covenant? Winthrop could say precisely—"It is by a mutual consent through a specially overruleing providence, and a more than ordinary approbation of the Churches of Christ to seeke out a place of Cohabitation and Consorteshipp under a due forme of Government both civill and ecclesiasticall." If it could be said thus concretely, why should there be any ambiguity? There was no doubt whatsoever about what Winthrop meant by a due form of ecclesiastical government: he meant the pure Biblical polity set forth in full detail by the New Testament, that method which later generations, in the days of increasing confusion, would settle down to calling Congregational, but which for Winthrop was no denominational peculiarity but the very essence of organized Christianity. What a due form of civil government meant, therefore, became crystal clear: a political regime, possessing power, which would consider its main function to be the erecting, protecting, and preserving of this form of polity. This due form would have, at the very beginning of its list of responsibilities, the duty of suppressing heresy, of subduing or somehow getting rid of dissenters—of being, in short, deliberately, vigorously, and consistently intolerant.

Regarded in this light, the Massachusetts Bay Company came on an errand in the second and later sense of the word: it was, so to speak, on its own business. What it set out to do was the sufficient reason for its setting out. About this Winthrop seems to be perfectly certain, as he declares specifically what the due forms will be attempting: the end is to improve our lives to do more service to the Lord, to increase the body of Christ, and to preserve our posterity from the corruptions of this evil world, so that they in turn shall work out their salvation under the purity and power of Biblical ordinances. Because the errand was so definable in advance, certain conclusions about the method of conducting it were equally evident: one, obviously, was that those sworn to the covenant should not be allowed to turn aside in a lust for mere physical rewards; but another was, in Winthrop's simple but splendid words, "we must be knit together in this worke as one man, wee must entertaine each other in brotherly affection." We must actually delight in each other, "always having before our eyes our Commission and community in the worke, our community as members of the same body." This was to say, were the great purpose kept steadily in mind, if all gazed only at it and strove only for it, then social solidarity (within a scheme of fixed and unalterable class distinctions) would be an automatic consequence. A society despatched upon an errand that is its own reward would want no other rewards: it could go forth to possess a land without ever becoming possessed by it; social gradations would remain eternally what God had originally appointed; there would be no internal contention among groups or interests, and though there would be hard work for everybody, prosperity would be bestowed not as a consequence of labor but as a sign of approval upon the mission itself. For once in the history of humanity (with all its sins), there would be a society so dedicated to a holy cause that success would prove innocent and triumph not raise up sinful pride or arrogant dissension.

Or, at least, this would come about if the people did not deal falsely with God, if they would live up to the articles of their bond. If we do not perform these terms, Winthrop warned, we may expect immediate manifestations of divine wrath; we shall perish out of the land we are crossing the sea to possess. And here in the 1660's and 1670's, all the jeremiads (of which Danforth's is one of the most poignant) are castigations of the people for having defaulted on precisely these articles. They recite the long list of afflictions an angry God had rained upon them, surely enough to prove how abysmally they had deserted the covenant: crop failures, epidemics, grasshoppers, caterpillars, torrid summers, arctic winters, Indian wars, hurricanes, shipwrecks, accidents, and (most grievous of all) unsatisfactory children. The solemn work of the election day, said Stoughton in 1668, is "Foundation-work"—not, that is, to lay a new one, "but to continue, and strengthen, and beautifie, and build upon that which has been laid." It had been laid in the covenant before even a foot was set ashore, and thereon New England should rest. Hence the terms of survival, let alone of prosperity, remained what had first been propounded:

"If we should so frustrate and deceive the Lords Expectations, that his Covenant-interest in us, and the Workings of his Salvation be made to cease, then All were lost indeed; Ruine upon Ruine, Destruction upon Destruction would come, until one stone were not left upon another."

Since so much of the literature after 1660—in fact just about all of it—dwells on this theme of declension and apostasy, would not the story of New England seem to be simply that of the failure of a mission? Winthrop's dread was realized: posterity had not found their salvation amid pure ordinances but had, despite the ordinances, yielded to the seductions of the good land. Hence distresses were being piled upon them, the slaughter of King Philip's War and now the attack of a profligate king upon the sacred charter. By about 1680, it did in truth seem that shortly no stone would be left upon another, that history would record of New England that the founders had been great men, but that their children and grandchildren progressively deteriorated.

This would certainly seem to be the impression conveyed by the assembled clergy and lay elders who, in 1679, met at Boston in a formal synod, under the leadership of Increase Mather, and there prepared a report on why the land suffered. The result of their deliberation, published under the title *The Necessity of Reformation,* was the first in what has proved to be a distressingly long succession of investigations into the civic health of Americans, and it is probably the most pessimistic. The land was afflicted, it said, because corruption had proceeded apace; assuredly, if the people did not quickly reform, the last blow would fall and nothing but desolation be left. Into what a moral quagmire this dedicated community had sunk, the synod did not leave to imagination; it published a long and detailed inventory of sins, crimes, misdemeanors, and nasty habits, which makes, to say the least, interesting reading.

We hear much talk nowadays about corruption, most of it couched in generalized terms. If we ask our current Jeremiahs to descend to particulars, they tell us that the republic is going on the rocks, or to the dogs, because the wives of politicians aspire to wear mink coats and their husbands take a moderate five per cent cut on certain deals to pay for the garments. The

Puritans were devotees of logic, and the verb "methodize" ruled their thinking. When the synod went to work, it had before it a succession of sermons, such as that of Danforth and the other election-day or fast-day orators, as well as such works as Increase Mather's *A Brief History of the Warr With the Indians*, wherein the decimating conflict with Philip was presented as a revenge upon the people for their transgressions. When the synod felt obliged to enumerate the enormities of the land so that the people could recognize just how far short of their errand they had fallen, it did not, in the modern manner, assume that regeneration would be accomplished at the next election by turning the rascals out, but it digested this body of literature; it reduced the contents to method. The result is a staggering compendium of inquiry, organized into twelve headings.

First, there was a great and visible decay of godliness. Second, there were several manifestations of pride—contention in the churches, insubordination of inferiors toward superiors, particularly of those inferiors who had, unaccountably, acquired more wealth than their betters, and, astonishingly, a shocking extravagance in attire, especially on the part of these of the meaner sort, who persisted in dressing beyond their means. Third, there were heretics, especially Quakers and Anabaptists. Fourth, a notable increase in swearing and a spreading disposition to sleep at sermons (these two phenomena seemed basically connected). Fifth, the Sabbath was wantonly violated. Sixth, family government had decayed, and fathers no longer kept their sons and daughters from prowling at night. Seventh, instead of people being knit together as one man in mutual love, they were full of contention, so that lawsuits were on the increase and lawyers were thriving. Under the eighth head, the synod described the sins of sex and alcohol, thus producing some of the juiciest prose of the period: militia days had become orgies, taverns were crowded; women threw temptation in way of befuddled men by wearing false locks and displaying naked necks and arms "or, which is more abominable, naked Breasts"; there were "mixed Dancings," along with light behavior and "Company-keeping" with vain persons, wherefore the bastardy rate was rising. In 1672, there was actually an attempt to supply Boston with a brothel (it was suppressed, but the synod was bearish about the future). Ninth, New Englanders were betraying a marked disposition to tell lies, especially when selling anything. In the tenth place, the business morality of even the most righteous left everything to be desired: the wealthy speculated in land and raised prices excessively; "Day-Labourers and Mechanicks are unreasonable in their demands." In the eleventh place, the people showed no disposition to reform, and in the twelfth, they seemed utterly destitute of civic spirit.

"The things here insisted on," said the synod, "have been often-times mentioned and inculcated by those whom the Lord hath set as Watchmen to the house of Israel." Indeed they had been, and thereafter they continued to be even more inculcated. At the end of the century, the synod's report was serving as a kind of handbook for preachers: they would take some verse of Isaiah or Jeremiah, set up the doctrine that God avenges the iniquities of a chosen people, and then run down the twelve heads, merely bringing the list up to date by inserting the new and still more depraved practices an ingenious people kept on devising. I suppose that in the whole literature of the world, including the satirists of imperial Rome, there is hardly such another uninhibited and unrelenting documentation of a people's descent into corruption.

I have elsewhere endeavored to argue that, while the social or economic historian may read this literature for its contents—and so construct from the expanding catalogue of denunciations a record of social progress—the cultural anthropologist will look slightly askance at these jeremiads; he will exercise a methodological caution about taking them at face value. If you read them all through, the total effect, curiously enough, is not at all depressing: you come to the paradoxical realization that they do not bespeak a despairing frame of mind. There is something of a ritualistic incantation about them; whatever they may signify in the realm of theology, in that of psychology they are purgations of soul; they do not discourage but actually encourage the community to persist in its heinous conduct. The exhortation to a reformation which never materializes serves as a token payment upon the obligation, and so liberates the debtors. Changes there had to be: adaptations to environment, expansion of the frontier, mansions constructed, commercial adventures undertaken. These activities were not specifically nominated in the bond Winthrop had framed. They were thrust upon the society by American experience; because they were not only works of necessity but of excitement, they proved irrestible—whether making money, haunting taverns, or committing fornication. Land speculation meant not only wealth but dispersion of the people, and what was to stop the march of settlement? The covenant doctrine preached on the *Arabella* has been formulated in England, where land was not to be had for the taking; its adherents had been utterly oblivious of what the fact of a frontier would do for an imported order, let alone for a European mentality. Hence I suggest that under the guise of this mounting wail of sinfulness, this incessant and never successful cry for repentance, the Puritans launched themselves upon the process of Americanization.

However, there are still more pertinent or more analytical things to be said of this body of expression. If you compare it with the great productions of the founders, you will be struck by the fact that the second and third generations had become oriented toward the social, and only the social, problem; herein they were deeply and profoundly different from their fathers. The finest creations of the founders—the disquisitions of Hooker, Shepard, and Cotton—were written in Europe, or else, if actually penned in the colonies, proceeded from a thoroughly European mentality, upon which the American scene made no impression whatsoever. The most striking example of this imperviousness is the poetry of Anne Bradstreet: she came to Massachusetts at the age of eighteen, already two years married to Simon Bradstreet; there, she says, "I found a new world and new manners, at which my heart rose" in rebellion, but soon convincing herself that it was the way of God, she submitted and joined the church. She bore Simon eight children, and loved him sincerely, as her most charming poem, addressed to him, reveals:

> *If ever two were one, then surely we;*
> *If ever man were loved by wife, then thee.*

After the house burned, she wrote a lament about how her pleasant things in ashes lay and how no more the merriment of guests would sound in the hall; but there is nothing in the poem to suggest that the house stood in North Andover or that the things so tragically consumed were doubly precious because they had been transported across the ocean and were utterly irreplaceable in the wilderness. In between rearing children and keeping house she wrote her poetry; her brother-in-law carried the manuscript to London, and there published it in 1650 under the ambitious title, *The Tenth Muse Lately Sprung Up in America.* But the title is the only thing about the volume which shows any sense of America, and that little merely in order to prove that the plantations had something in the way of European wit and learning, that they had not receded into barbarism. Anne's flowers are English flowers, the birds, English birds, and the landscape is Lincolnshire. So also with the productions of immigrant scholarship: such a learned and acute work as Hooker's *Survey of the Summe of Church Discipline,* which is specifically about the regime set up in America, is written entirely within the logical patterns, and out of the religious experience, of Europe; it makes no concession to new and peculiar circumstances.

The titles alone of productions in the next generation show how concentrated have become emotion and attention upon the interest of New England, and none is more revealing than Samuel Danforth's conception of an errand into the wilderness. Instead of being able to compose abstract treatises like those of Hooker upon the soul's preparation, humiliation, or exultation, or such a collection of wisdom and theology as John Cotton's *The Way of Life* or Shepard's *The Sound Believer,* these later saints must, over and over again, dwell upon the specific sins of New England, and the more they denounce, the more they must narrow their focus to the provincial problem. If they write upon anything else, it must be about the halfway covenant and its manifold consequences—a development enacted wholly in this country— or else upon their wars with the Indians. Their range is sadly constricted, but every effort, no matter how brief, is addressed to the persistent question: what is the meaning of this society in the wilderness? If it does not mean what Winthrop said it must mean, what under Heaven is it? Who, they are forever asking themselves, who are we?—and sometimes they are on the verge of saying, who the Devil are we, anyway?

This brings us back to the fundamental ambiguity concealed in the word "errand," that *double entente* of which I am certain Danforth was aware when he published the words that give point to the exhibition. While it was true that in 1630, the covenant philosophy of a special and peculiar bond lifted the migration out of the ordinary realm of nature, provided it with a definite mission which might in the secondary sense be called its errand, there was always present in Puritan thinking the suspicion that God's saints are at best inferiors, despatched by their Superior upon particular assignments. Anyone who has run errands for other people, particularly for people of great importance with many things on their minds, such as army commanders, knows how real is the peril that, by the time he returns with the report of a message delivered or a bridge blown up, the Superior may be interested in something else; the situation at headquarters may be entirely changed, and the gallant errand boy, or the husband who desperately remembered to buy the ribbon, may be told that he is too late. This tragic pattern appears again and again in modern warfare: an agent is dropped by parachute and, after immense hardships, comes back to find that, in the shifting tactical or strategic situations, his contribution is no longer of value. If he gets home in time and his service proves useful, he receives a medal; otherwise, no matter what prodigies he has performed, he may not even be thanked. He has been sent, as the devastating phrase has it, upon a fool's errand, than which there can be a no more shattering blow to self-esteem.

The Great Migration of 1630 felt insured against such treatment from on high by the covenant; nevertheless, the God of the covenant always remained an unpredictable Jehovah, a *Deus Absconditus*. When God promises to abide by stated terms, His word, of course, is to be trusted; but then, what is man that he dare accuse Omnipotence of tergiversation? But if any such apprehension was in Winthrop's mind as he spoke on the *Arabella*, or in the minds of other apologists for the enterprise, they kept it far back and allowed it no utterance. They could stifle the thought, not only because Winthrop and his colleagues believed fully in the covenant, but because they could see in the pattern of history that their errand was not a mere scouting expedition:

it was an essential maneuver in the drama of Christendom. The Bay Company was not a battered remnant of suffering Separatists thrown up on a rocky shore; it was an organized task force of Christians, executing a flank attack on the corruptions of Christendom. These Puritans did not flee to America; they went in order to work out that complete reformation which was not yet accomplished in England and Europe, but which would quickly be accomplished if only the saints back there had a working model to guide them. It is impossible to say that any who sailed from Southampton really expected to lay his bones in the new world; were it to come about—as all in their heart of hearts anticipated—that the forces of righteousness should prevail against Laud and Wentworth, that England after all should turn toward reformation, where else would the distracted country look for leadership except to those who in New England had perfected the ideal polity and who would know how to administer it? This was the large unspoken assumption in the errand of 1630: if the conscious intention were realized, not only would a federated Jehovah bless the new land, but He would bring back these temporary colonials to govern England.

In this respect, therefore, we may say that the migration was running an errand in the earlier and more primitive sense of the word—performing a job not so much for Jehovah as for history, which was the wisdom of Jehovah expressed through time. Winthrop was aware of this aspect of the mission—fully conscious of it. "For wee must Consider that wee shall be as a Citty upon a Hill, the eies of all people are uppon us." More was at stake than just one little colony. If we deal falsely with God, not only will He descend upon us in wrath, but even more terribly, He will make us "a story and a by-word through the world, wee shall open the mouthes of enemies to speake evill of the wayes of god and all professours for Gods sake." No less than John Milton was New England to justify God's ways to man, though not, like him, in the agony and confusion of defeat but in the confidence of approaching triumph. This errand was being run for the sake of Reformed Christianity; and while the first aim was indeed to realize in America the due form of government, both civil and ecclesiastical, the aim behind that aim was to vindicate the most rigorous ideal of the Reformation, so that ultimately all Europe would imitate New England. If we succeed, Winthrop told his audience, men will say of later plantations, "the lord make it like that of New England." There was an elementary prudence to be observed: Winthrop said that the prayer would arise from subsequent plantations, yet what was England itself but one of God's plantations? In America, he promised, we shall see, or may see, more of God's wisdom, power, and truth "then formerly wee have beene acquainted with." The situation was such that, for the moment, the model had no chance to be exhibited in England; Puritans could talk about it, theorize upon it, but they could not display it, could not prove that it would actually work. But if they had it set up in America—in a bare land, devoid of already established (and corrupt) institutions, empty of bishops and courtiers, where they could start *de novo,* and the eyes of the world were upon it—and if then it performed just as the saints had predicted of it, the Calvinist internationale would know exactly how to go about completing the already begun but temporarily stalled revolution in Europe.[1]

When we look upon the enterprise from this point of view, the psychology of the second and third generations becomes more comprehensible. We realize that the migration was not sent upon its errand in order to found the United States of America, nor even the New England conscience. Actually, it would not perform its errand even when the colonists did erect a due form of government in church and state: what was further required in order for this mission to be a success was that the eyes of the world be kept fixed upon it in rapt attention. If the rest of the world, or at least of Protestantism, looked elsewhere, or turned to another model, or simply got distracted and forgot about New England, if the new land was left with a policy nobody in the great world of Europe wanted—then every success in fulfilling the terms of the covenant would become a diabolical measure of

---

[1] See the perceptive analysis of Alan Heimert *(The New England Quarterly,* XXVI, September 1953) of the ingredients that ultimately went into the Puritans' metaphor of the "wilderness," all the more striking a concoction because they attached no significance a priori to their wilderness destination. To begin with, it was simply a void.

failure. If the due form of government were not everywhere to be saluted, what would New England have upon its hands? How give it a name, this victory nobody could utilize? How provide an identity for something conceived under misapprehensions? How could a universal which turned out to be nothing but a provincial particular be called anything but a blunder or an abortion?

If an actor, playing the leading role in the greatest dramatic spectacle of the century, were to attire himself and put on his make-up, rehearse his lines, take a deep breath, and stride onto the stage, only to find the theater dark and empty, no spotlight working, and himself entirely alone, he would feel as did New England around 1650 or 1660. For in the 1640's, during the Civil Wars, the colonies, so to speak, lost their audience. First of all, there proved to be, deep in the Puritan movement, an irreconcilable split between the Presbyterian and Independent wings, wherefore no one system could be imposed upon England, and so the New England model was unserviceable. Secondly—most horrible to relate—the Independents, who in polity were carrying New England's banner and were supposed, in the schedule of history, to lead England into imitation of the colonial order, betrayed the sacred cause by yielding to the heresy of toleration. They actually welcomed Roger Williams, whom the leaders of the model had kicked out of Massachusetts so that his nonsense about liberty of conscience would not spoil the administrations of charity.

In other words, New England did not lie, did not falter; it made good everything Winthrop demanded—wonderfully good—and then found that its lesson was rejected by those choice spirits for whom the exertion had been made. By casting out Williams, Anne Hutchinson, and the Antinomians, along with an assortment of Gortonists and Anabaptists, into that cesspool then becoming known as Rhode Island, Winthrop, Dudley, and the clerical leaders showed Oliver Cromwell how he should go about governing England. Instead, he developed the utterly absurd theory that so long as a man made a good soldier in the New Model Army, it did not matter whether he was a Calvinist, an Antinomian, an Arminian, an Anabaptist or even—horror of horrors—a Socinian! Year after year, as the circus tours this country, crowds howl with laughter, no matter how many times they have seen the stunt, at the bustle that walks by itself: the clown comes out dressed in a large skirt with a bustle behind; he turns sharply to the left, and the bustle continues blindly and obstinately straight ahead, on the original course. It is funny in a circus, but not in history. There is nothing but tragedy in' the realization that one was in the main path of events, and now is sidetracked and disregarded. One is always able, of course, to stand firm on his first resolution, and to condemn the clown of history for taking the wrong turning: yet this is a desolating sort of stoicism, because it always carries with it the recognition that history will never come back to the predicted path, and that with one's own demise, righteousness must die out of the world.

The most humiliating element in the experience was the way the English brethren turned upon the colonials for precisely their greatest achievement. It must have seemed, for those who came with Winthrop in 1630 and who remembered the clarity and brilliance with which he set forth the conditions of their errand, that the world was turned upside down and inside out when, in June 1645, thirteen leading Independent divines—such men as Goodwin, Owen, Nye, Burroughs, formerly friends and allies of Hooker and Davenport, men who might easily have come to New England and helped extirpate heretics—wrote the General Court that the colony's law banishing Anabaptists was an embarrassment to the Independent cause in England. Opponents were declaring, said these worthies, "that persons of our way, principall and spirit cannot beare with Dissentors from them, but Doe correct, fine, imprison and banish them wherever they have power soe to Doe." There were indeed people in England who admired the severities of Massachusetts, but we assure you, said the Independents, these "are utterly your enemyes and Doe seeke your extirpation from the face of the earth: those who now in power are your friends are quite otherwise minded, and doe professe they are much offended with your proceedings." Thus early commenced that chronic weakness in the foreign policy of Americans, an inability to recognize who in truth constitute their best friends abroad.

We have lately accustomed ourselves to the fact that there does exist a mentality which will take advantage of the liberties allowed by society in order to conspire for the ultimate suppression of those same privileges. The government of Charles I and Archbishop Laud had not, where that danger was concerned, been liberal, but it had been conspicuously inefficient; hence, it did not liquidate the Puritans (although it made halfhearted efforts), nor did it herd them into prison camps. Instead, it generously, even lavishly, gave a group of them a charter to Massachusetts Bay, and obligingly left out the standard clause requiring that the document remain in London, that the grantees keep their office within reach of Whitehall. Winthrop's revolutionaries availed themselves of this liberty to get the charter overseas, and thus to set up a regime dedicated to the worship of God in the manner they desired—which meant allowing nobody else to worship any other way, especially adherents of Laud and King Charles. All this was perfectly logical and consistent. But what happened to the thought processes of their fellows in England made no sense whatsoever. Out of the New Model Army came the fantastic notion that a party struggling for power should proclaim that, once it captured the state, it would recognize the right of dissenters to disagree and to have their own worship, to hold their own opinions. Oliver Cromwell was so far gone in this idiocy as to became a dictator, in order to impose toleration by force! Amid this shambles, the errand of New England collapsed. There was nobody left at headquarters to whom reports could be sent.

Many a man has done a brave deed, been hailed as a public hero, had honors and ticker tape heaped upon him—and then had to live, day after day, in the ordinary routine, eating breakfast and brushing his teeth, in what seems protracted anticlimax. A couple may win their way to each other across insuperable obstacles, elope in a blaze of passion and glory—and then have to learn that life is a matter of buying the groceries and getting the laundry done. This sense of the meaning having gone out of life, that all adventures are over, that no great days and no heroism lie ahead, is particularly galling when it falls upon a son whose father once was the public hero or the great lover. He has to put up with the daily routine without ever having known at first hand the thrill of danger or the ecstasy of passion.

True, he has his own hardships—clearing rocky pastures, hauling in the cod during a storm, fighting Indians in a swamp—but what are these compared with the magnificence of leading an exodus of saints to found a city on a hill, for the eyes of all the world to behold? He might wage a stout fight against the Indians, and one out of ten of his fellows might perish in the struggle, but the world was no longer interested. He would be reduced to writing accounts of himself and scheming to get a publisher in London, in a desperate effort to tell a heedless world, "Look, I exist!"

His greatest difficulty would be not the stones, storms, and Indians, but the problem of his identity. In something of this sort, I should like to suggest, consists the anxiety and torment that inform productions of the late seventeenth and early eighteenth centuries—and should I say, some thereafter? It appears most clearly in *Magnalia Christi Americana,* the work of that soul most tortured by the problem, Cotton Mather: "I write the Wonders of the Christian Religion, flying from the Depravations of Europe, to the American Strand." Thus he proudly begins, and at once trips over the acknowledgment that the founders had not simply fled from depraved Europe but had intended to redeem it. And so the book is full of lamentations over the declension of the children, who appear, page after page, in contrast to their mighty progenitors, about as profligate a lot as ever squandered a great inheritance.

And yet, the *Magnalia* is not an abject book; neither are the election sermons abject, nor is the inventory of sins offered by the synod of 1679. There is bewilderment, confusion, chagrin, but there is no surrender. A task has been assigned upon which the populace are in fact intensely engaged. But they are not sure any more for just whom they are working; they know they are moving, but they do not know where they are going. They seem still to be on an errand, but if they are no longer inferiors sent by the superior forces of the Reformation, to whom they should report, then their errand must be wholly of the second sort, something with a purpose and an intention sufficient unto itself. If so, what is it? If it be not the due form of government, civil and ecclesiastical, that they brought into being, how otherwise can it be described?

The literature of self-condemnation must be read for meanings far below the surface, for meanings of which, we may be so rash as to surmise, the authors were not fully conscious, but by which they were troubled and goaded. They looked in vain to history for an explanation of themselves; more and more it appeared that the meaning was not to be found in theology, even with the help of the covenantal dialectic. Thereupon, these citizens found that they had no other place to search but within themselves—even though, at first sight, that repository appeared to be nothing but a sink of iniquity. Their errand having failed in the first sense of the term, they were left with the second, and required to fill it with meaning by themselves and out of themselves. Having failed to rivet the eyes of the world upon their city on the hill, they were left alone with America.

13   *Edward Johnson*

Wonder-Working Providence of Sions Saviour

The sense of mission was frequently expressed as a belief that New England was destined to be a new Canaan. The disappointments of the 1640's by no means eliminated the feeling that the American Puritans had a special role to play. This conviction was expressed most often in the histories of the settlement of the Bay colony which began to appear quite early.

Captain Edward Johnson was one of the founders and the leading citizen of the town of Woburn, Massachusetts. In 1653 he published his History of New England *(also known as* Johnson's Wonder-Working Providence) *to defend the reputation of Massachusetts. In it he demonstrated how God had affirmed the special errand of New England by the miraculous assistance he gave to the endeavors of the American Puritans.*

SOURCE. Edward Johnson, "Wonder-Working Providence of Sions Saviour," in *Johnson's Wonder Working Providence, 1628–1651,* J. Franklin Jameson, ed *The Original Narratives of Early American History,* unnumbered volume. New York: Charles Scribner's Sons, 1910, pp. 23–25. Reprinted by permission of Barnes & Noble, Inc.

WONDER-WORKING PROVIDENCE OF SIONS SAVIOUR

Being a Relation of the First Planting in New England,
In the Yeare, 1628

The sad Condition of England, when this People removed

When England began to decline in Religion, like lukewarme Laodicea, and instead of purging out Popery, a farther compliance was sought not onely in vaine Idolatrous Ceremonies but also in prophaning the Sabbath, and by Proclamation throughout their Parish churches, exasperating lewd and prophane persons to celebrate a Sabbath like the Heathen to Venus, Baccus and Ceres, in so much that the multitude of irreligious, lascivious and popish affected persons spred the whole land like Grashoppers; in this very time Christ the glorious King of his Churches raises an Army out of our English Nation, for freeing his people from their long servitude under usurping Prelacy; and because every corner of England was filled with the fury of malignant adversaries, Christ creates a New England to muster up the first of his Forces in; Whose low condition, little number, and remotenesse of place made these adversaries triumph, despising this day of small things, but in this hight of their pride the Lord Christ brought sudden, and unexpected destruction upon them. Thus have you a touch of the time when this worke began.

Christ Jesus, intending to manifest his Kingly Office toward his Churches more fully than ever yet the Sons of men saw, even to the uniting of Jew and Gentile Churches in one Faith, begins with our English Nation (whose former reformation being very imperfect) doth now resolve to cast down their false foundation of Prelacy, even in the hight of their domineering dignity. And therefore in the yeere 1628, he stirres up his servants as the Heralds of a King to make this proclamation for Voluntiers, as followeth.

"Oh yes! Oh yes! Oh yes! All you the people of Christ that are here Oppressed, Imprisoned and scurrilously derided, gather yourselves together, your Wives and little ones, and answer to your severall Names as you shall be shipped for his service, in the Westerne World, and more especially for planting the united Collonies of new England, Where you are to attend the service of the King of Kings."

Upon the divulging of this Proclamation by his Herralds at Armes, many (although otherwise willing for this service) began to object as followeth:

"Can it possible be the mind of Christ, (who formerly in-abled so many Souldiers of his to keepe their station unto the death here) that now so many brave Souldiers disciplined by Christ himselfe, the Captaine of our salvation, should turne their backs to the disheartning of their Fellow-Souldiers, and losse of Further opportunity in gaining a greater number of Subjects to Christs Kingdome?"

Notwithstanding this Objection, it was further proclaimed as followeth: "What, Creature, wilt not know that Christ thy King crusheth with a rod of Iron, the Pompe and Pride of man, and must he like man cast and contrive to take his enemies at advantage? No, of purpose hee causeth such instruments to retreate as hee hath made strong for himselfe: that so his adversaries, glorying in the pride of their power, insulting over the little remnant remaining, Christ causeth them to be cast downe suddenly forever, and wee find in stories reported, Earths Princes have passed their Armies at need over Seas and deepe Torrents. Could Caesar so suddenly fetch over forces from Europe to Asia, Pompy to foyle? How much more shall Christ who createth all power, call over this 900 league Ocean at his pleasure, such instruments as he thinks meete to make use of in this place, from whence you are now to depart, but further that you may not delay the Voyage intended, for your full satisfaction, know this is the place where the Lord will create a new Heaven, and a new Earth in, new Churches, and a new Common-wealth together."

14   Roger Williams

American Exceptionalism Rejected

Roger Williams' disagreements with the founders of the Bay Colony were not limited to his unusual attitude toward state-church relations. He emphatically rejected the idea that the American Puritans had a special, divinely ordained errand from God. For Williams it was impossible for any community as a whole to be covenanted with God. In rejecting the Puritan sense of mission, Williams was speaking for almost no one in New England but himself. Yet in this, as in many things, Williams reveals the contradictions inherent in the orthodox attitude. In arguing that Christianity, unlike ancient Judaism, could not be identified in any way with a particular location or group of people, Williams exposed the implicit contradiction between the belief that the Puritans were a chosen people and the universal purpose for which they had been chosen.

The deepest of all Puritan legacies has been the conviction that this nation is ultimately exceptional. At the beginning of American history Williams rejected the idea that America was in any fundamental way exempt from the natural and social forces that affected the destinies of all peoples. In this one sense, at least, he resembled the contemporary American radicals who reject our national claims to a unique destiny.

The Scriptures, or writings of truth, are those heavenly righteous scales, wherein all our controversies must be tried, and that blessed Starre that leads all those soules to Jesus that seek him. But saith Mr. Cotton, two of those Scriptures alleged by me (Isa. 52.11., Revel. 18.4. which I brought to prove a necessitie of leaving the false, before a joyning to the true Church) they

SOURCE. Roger Williams, "American Exceptionalism Rejected" from *Mr. Cotton's Letter Lately Printed, Examined and Answered,* Vol. I, Reuben Aldridge Guild, ed., *The Complete Writings of Roger Williams,* (1866), Perry Miller, ed. New York: Russell & Russell, 1963, pp. 359–361. Reprinted by permission of the publisher.

speake of locall separation, which (saith he) your selfe know we have made.

For that locall and typicall separation from Babylon, Isa. 52., I could not well have beleeved that Mr. Cotton, or any, would make that comming forth of Babel in the Antitype, Rev. 18. 4. to be locall and materiall also. What civill State, Nation or Countrey in the world, in the antitype, must now be called Babel? Certainly, if any, then Babel is it selfe properly so called: but there we find (as before) a true Church. of Jesus Christ, 1 Pet. 5.

Secondly, if Babel be locall now, whence Gods people are called, then must there be a locall Judea, a Land of Canaan also, into which they are called. And where shall both that Babel and Canaan be found in all the commings forth that have been made from the Church of Rome in these last times? But Mr. Cotton having made a locall departure from Old England in Europe, to New England in America, can he satisfie his owne soule, or the soules of other men, that he hath obeyed that voice, come out of Babel my people, partake not of her sins, &c. Doth he count the very Land of England literally Babel, and so consequently Egypt and Sodome, Revel. 11. 8. and the Land of new England, Judea, Canaan? &c.

The Lord Jesus (John 4.) clearly breaks down all difference of places, and Acts 10. all differences of persons.

PART SIX

New Approaches

15   *Michael Walzer*

Puritan Repression and Modernization

The relationship, if any, between Puritanism and some of the components of "modernism," such as liberalism, capitalism, democracy, and science, has fascinated historians at least since the beginning of this century when the great German sociologist Max Weber argued that Puritanism played an important role in the development of modern economic life. No question of comparable scope has been of more persistent interest in recent historiography. Although most of the writing on the various aspects of this problem has been based on the study of English Puritanism, some, particularly in regard to the origins of democracy, has been focused on New England and all of it is relevant to colonial America.

Michael Walzer, a young social scientists at Harvard University, holds that Puritanism must be understood both as a movement peculiar to the seventeenth century and as a factor in the modernization of the west in his important book, The Revolution of the Saints: A Study in the Origins of Radical Politics. *Using a psychological approach, he deals with the complex relationship between individual personality and social development and argues that Puritanism was at once a response to and an instrument of change.*

SOURCE. Reprinted by permission of publishers from Michael Walzer, *The Revolution of the Saints: A Study in the Origins of Radical Politics*, pp. 300–316. Cambridge, Mass.: Harvard University Press. Copyright 1965 by the President and Fellows of Harvard College.

Virtually all the modern world has been read into Calvinism: liberal politics and voluntary association; capitalism and the social discipline upon which it rests; bureaucracy with its systematic procedures and its putatively diligent and devoted officials; and finally all the routine forms of repression, joylessness, and unrelaxed aspiration. By one or another writer, the faith of the brethren, and especially of the Puritan brethren, has been made the source or cause or first embodiment of the most crucial elements of modernity. Undoubtedly there is some truth in all these interpretations . . . . It is now necessary to add, however, that this incorporation was a long and complex process, involving selection, corruption, and transformation; it was the result of men *working upon* their Calvinist heritage. Calvinism in its sixteenth- and seventeenth-century forms was not so much the cause of this or that modern economic, political, or administrative system as it was an agent of modernization, an ideology of the transition period. And as the conditions of crisis and upheaval in which Calvinism was conceived and developed did not persist, so Calvinism as an integral and creative force did not endure. It gave way to other social and intellectual forces which sustained something of its achievement but not everything—indeed, very far from everything.

Calvinism was not a liberal ideology, even though congregational life was surely a training for self-government and democratic participation. The radically democratic Levellers probably had their beginning in the Puritan congregations, in the debates, for example, that preceded the elections of ministers and in the recriminations that so frequently followed. Even when the choice of ministers was not open to the church membership, as it often was not, politics in the congregation was very different from the influence, intrigue, and patronage that prevailed at the bishop's or the king's court. Personal loyalty and deference, so highly developed among the courtiers, declined among the brethren. Calvinist voluntarism established instead the freely negotiated contract as the highest human bond; in its terms, Puritan writers described the connection of man and God, of the saint and his associates, of minister and church, of husband and wife. All these relations were entered into willingly and knowingly, and if men were thus to negotiate contracts they obviously required some knowledge of the contract's content and purposes. The preaching and writing of the ministers was designed to provide such knowledge; so was the discussion among lay Puritans of the sermons and the texts; so also the congregational debates, the reading, note taking and diary-keeping of the newly political, newly educated saints. And all this was preparation also for the debates and elections, the pamphlets and parties of liberal politics.

But Puritanism was much more than this, as the previous description of the "attack upon the traditional world" and the "new world of discipline and work" ought to have made clear. The associations of the brethren were voluntary indeed, but they gave rise to a collectivist discipline marked above all by a tense mutual "watchfulness." Puritan individualism never led to a respect for privacy. Tender conscience had its rights, but it was protected only against the interference of worldlings and not against "brotherly admonition." And the admonitions of the brethren were anxious, insistent, continuous. They felt themselves to be living in an age of chaos and crime and sought to train conscience to be permanently on guard, permanently at war, against sin. Debate in a Puritan congregation was never a free and easy exchange of ideas; the need for vigilance, the pressures of war were too great to allow for friendly disagreement. What lay behind the warfare of the saints? Two things above all: a fierce antagonism to the traditional world and the prevailing pattern of human relation and a keen and perhaps not unrealistic anxiety about human wickedness and the dangers of social disorder. The saints attempted to fasten upon the necks of all mankind the yoke of a new political discipline—impersonal and ideological, not founded upon loyalty or affection, no more open to spontaneity than to chaos and crime. This discipline was not to depend upon the authority of paternal kings and lords or upon the obedience of childlike and trustful subjects. Puritans sought to make it voluntary, like the contract itself, the object of individual and collective willfulness. But voluntary or not, its keynote was repression.

Liberalism also required such voluntary subjection and self-control, but in sharp contrast to Puritanism, its politics was shaped by an extraordinary confidence in the possibility of both, a firm sense of human reasonableness and of the relative ease with which order might be attained. Liberal confidence made repression and the endless struggle against sin unnecessary; it also tended to make self-control invisible, that is, to forget its painful history and naively assume its existence. The result was that liberalism did not create the self-control it required. The Lockeian state was not a disciplinary institution as was the Calvinist holy commonwealth, but rather rested on the assumed political virtue of its citizens. It is one of the central arguments of this conclusion that Puritan repression has its place in the practical history of that strange assumption.

It is not possible to judge in any absolute terms the effectiveness of this repression or the extent of the social need for it. It can only be said that the Puritans *knew about* human sinfulness and that Locke did not need to know. This undoubtedly reflects not only different temperaments but also different experiences. The very existence and spread of Puritanism in the years before the revolution surely suggest the presence in English society of an acute fear of disorder and "wickedness"—a fear, it has been argued above, attendant upon the transformation of the old political and social order. The triumph of Lockeian ideas, on the other hand, suggests the overcoming of anxiety, the appearance of saints and citizens for whom sin is no longer a problem. The struggle against the old order seems largely to have been won by Locke's time, and the excitement, confusion, and fearfulness of that struggle almost forgotten. Lockeian liberals found it possible to dispense with religious, even with ideological, controls in human society and thought enthusiasm and battle-readiness unattractive. But this was only because the controls had already been implanted *in men*. In a sense, then, liberalism was dependent upon the existence of "saints," that is, of persons whose good behavior could be relied upon. At the same time, the secular and genteel character of liberalism was determined by the fact that these were "saints" whose goodness (sociability, moral decency, or mere respectability) was self-assured and relaxed, free from the nervousness and fanaticism of Calvinist godliness.

This, then, is the relation of Puritanism to the liberal world: it is perhaps one of historical preparation, but not at all of theoretical contribution. Indeed, there was much to be forgotten and much to be surrendered before the saint could become a liberal bourgeois. During the great creative period of English Puritanism, the faith of the saints and the tolerant reasonableness of the liberals had very little in common.

Roughly the same things can be said about the putative connection of Calvinism and capitalism. The moral discipline of the saints can be interpreted as the historical conditioning of the capitalist man; but the discipline was not itself capitalist. It can be argued that the faith of the brethren, with its emphasis upon methodical endeavor and self-control, was an admirable preparation for systematic work in shops, offices, and factories. It trained men for the minute-to-minute attentiveness required in a modern economic system; it taught them to forego their afternoon naps—as they had but recently foregone their saint's day holidays—and to devote spare hours to bookkeeping and moral introspection. It somehow made the deprivation and repression inevitable in sustained labor bearable and even desirable for the saints. And by teaching self-control, it provided the basis for impersonal, contractual relations among men, allowing workmanlike cooperation but not involving any exchange of affection or any of the risks of intimacy. All this, Calvinism did or helped to do. Whether it did so in a creative fashion or as the ideological reflection of new economic processes is not immediately relevant. The saints learned, as Weber has suggested, a kind of rational and worldly asceticism, and this was probably something more than the economic routine required. They sought in work itself what mere work can never give: a sense of vocation and discipline that would free them from sinfulness and the fear of disorder.

But Weber has said more than this; he has argued that systematic acquisition as well as asceticism has a Calvinist origin. The psychological tension induced by the theory of predestination, working itself out in worldly activity, presumably drove men to seek success as a sign of salvation. The sheer willfulness of an inscrutable God produced in its turn, if Weber is correct, the willfulness of an anxious man and set off the entrepreneurial pursuit of better business techniques and more and more profit. At this point his argument breaks down. If there is in fact a peculiar and irrational quality to the capitalists' lust for gain, its sources must be sought elsewhere than among the saints. For Puritanism was hardly an ideology that encouraged continuous or unrestrained accumulation. Instead, the saints tended to be narrow and conservative in their economic views, urging men to seek no more wealth than they needed for a modest life, or, alternatively, to use up their surplus in charitable giving. The anxiety of the Puritans led to a fearful demand for economic restriction (and political control) rather than to entrepreneurial actively as Weber has described it. Unremitting and relatively unremunerative work was the greatest help toward saintliness and virtue.

The ideas of Puritan writers are here very close to those of such proto-Jacobins as Mably and Morelly in eighteenth-century France, who also watched the development of capitalist enterprise with unfriendly eyes, dreaming of a spartan republic where bankers and great merchants would be unwelcome. The collective discipline of the Puritans—their Christian Sparta—was equally incompatible with purely acquisitive activity. Virtue would almost certainly require economic regulation. This would be very different from the regulation of medieval corporatism and perhaps it was the first sense of that difference that received the name *freedom*. It was accompanied by a keen economic realism: thus the Calvinist acknowledgment of the lawfulness of usury. But Calvinist realism was in the service of effective control and not of free activity or self-expression. Who can doubt that, had the holy commonwealth ever been firmly established, godly self-discipline and mutual surveillance would have been far more repressive than the corporate system? Once again, in the absence of a Puritan state the discipline was enforced through the congregation. The minutes of a seventeenth-century consistory provide a routine example: "The church was satisfied with Mrs. Carlton," they read, "as to the weight of her butter." Did Mrs. Carlton tremble, awaiting that verdict? Surely if the brethren were unwilling to grant liberty to the local butter-seller, they would hardly have granted it to the new capitalist. The ministerial literature, at least, is full of denunciations of enclosures, usurers, monopolists, and projectors—and occasionally even of wily merchants. Puritan casuistry, perhaps, left such men sufficient room in which to range, but it hardly offered them what Weber considers so essential—a good conscience. Only a sustained endeavor in hypocrisy could have earned them that. The final judgment of the saints with regard to the pursuit of money is that of Bunyan's pilgrim, angry and ill-at-ease in the town of Vanity, disdainful of such companions as Mr. Money-love and Mr. Save-all.

Liberalism and capitalism appear fully developed only in a secular form, that is, only after Puritanism is spent as a creative force. It seems likely that a certain freedom from religious controls and religious scruples is essential for their general triumph in modern Western society. This freedom may well have its origins in the Reformation, in the attack upon the established church and the traditional priesthood, but it was not the responsibility of the reformers; it lay beyond their intentions. The holy commonwealth would have been neither liberal nor capitalist—no more, indeed, than would the Jacobin Republic of Virtue. The spread of the capitalist and liberal spirits parallels the decline of radical enthusiasm. At the same time, however, radical enthusiasm in the years before its decline helped to shape the disciplinary basis of the new economy and politics. In a sense, worldly asceticism preceded entrepreneurial freedom, just as political zeal preceded liberalism. There is an historical interdependence, not easy to understand though vulgar moralists have made it a cliché, between discipline and liberty—or rather, between discipline and a certain sort of liberty.

Neither Max Weber nor any of his followers have ever demonstrated that the Englishmen who actually became Puritans, who really believed in predestination and lived through the salvation panic, went on to become capitalist businessmen. The burden of the evidence would seem to be against such a conclusion, though this is not certain; it is possible that businessmen are simply less likely to keep records of their spiritual struggles than of their economic affairs. The weight of such diaries, letters, and memoirs as we possess, however, suggests that the most significant expression of the new faith was cultural and political rather than economic. The saints were indeed activists, and activists in a far more intense and "driven" fashion than the men who came later: English gentlemen after their conversions attended to parliamentary affairs with a new assiduousness; pious mothers trained their sons to a constant concern with political life; enthusiastic apprentices took notes at sermons and studied the latest religious and political pamphlets. The outcome of Puritan activity was godly watchfulness, magistracy, and revolution.

Had the revolution succeeded, the discipline of the holy commonwealth, as of the Jacobin Republic of Virtue, would have required an institutionalized political activism. Each utopia would have proliferated a petty officialdom, a host of minor administrators busily enforcing the new rules and regulations. The ideas of John Eliot of Massachusetts suggest an image of the holy commonwealth as an over-governed society, with every tenth man an official. These zealous and conscientious magistrates—equipped with a realistic and intolerant sense of the sinfulness of their fellow men—would hardly constitute a modern bureaucracy, though once again their religious contentiousness may suggest the difficult, half-forgotten origins of modern bureaucratic discipline. The zeal of the saints seems to have little in common with the secular competence, functional rationality, and moderate devotion required of modern officials. Yet magistracy is a far better description of the saints' true vocation than is either capitalist acquisition or bourgeois freedom. It suggests most clearly the activist role that Puritanism called upon the saints to play in the creation and maintenance of a new moral order. This activity was political in the sense that it was always concerned with government—though not only or most importantly at the level of the state. For Puritans imagined the congregation as a "little commonwealth," debated worriedly over its constitution and sought means to discipline recalcitrant members; they saw the family as a voluntary community dominated by a godly father whom they described as a governor. And finally, they saw the self as a divided being, spirit at war with flesh, and there also they sought control and government.

Once Calvinism and Puritanism have been described in the political language of repression and war it becomes easier to answer the question posed in the first chapter of this book: why did particular groups of Englishmen and Frenchmen, Scots and Dutchman become Calvinists and Puritans? They did so, it may be suggested, because they felt some need for the self-control and godly government that sainthood offered. This is to push Weber's explanation of capitalism a step further back: he has argued that Calvinism was an anxiety-inducing ideology that drove its adherents to seek a sense of control and confidence in methodical work and worldly success. But he has not even raised the question of why men should adopt an anxiety-inducing ideology in the first place, a question to which his own concept of "elective affinity" offers a possible answer. Now it is probably not true that Calvinism *induced* anxiety; more likely its effect was to confirm and explain in theological terms perceptions men already had of the dangers of the world and the self. But what made Calvinism an "appropriate" option for anxiety-ridden individuals was not only this confirmation, but also the fact that sainthood offered a way out of anxiety. Puritan "method" led to tranquillity and assurance through the "exercises" of self-control and spiritual warfare, and it then led to the political order of the holy commonwealth through the corresponding "exercises" of magistracy and revolution.

Men were likely to become saints, or rather, it is understandable that certain men should have become saints, if their social and personal experiences had been of a certain sort. Three different sets of experiences have been discussed in the preceding pages: that of discontented and fearful noblemen like the French Huguenots who sought some way to adjust to a modern political order; that of clerical intellectuals, newly freed from corporate ties (and from the privileges that went along with those ties) and especially sensitive to the ambiguities of their own position and the disorder of their society; and finally that of new or newly educated gentlemen, lawyers and merchants, nervously making their way in university, parliament, and city, with a claim to stake in the political and social worlds. None of these group experiences make individual conversion predictable; each of them makes it comprehensible. Thus the moderate Calvinism of a man like Philip de Mornay can be viewed as the willful effort of an educated and ambitious French gentleman to demonstrate to himself as well as to others his worthiness for political offce—a demonstration that required a rigid rejection of Renaissance pleasure and extravagance. The fanatical self-righteousness of that first Puritan John Knox, a Scottish peasant's son set loose in Europe by war and revolution, can best be understood as in some sense a function of his exile. Righteousness was a consolation and a way of organizing the self for survival. When John Whitgift, the future archbishop, cruelly taunted Thomas Cartwright for "eating at other men's tables," he was perhaps suggesting an important source of Cartwright's ideas of congregational unity and ministerial status. And finally, it can be argued, country gentlemen like John Winthrop and Oliver Cromwell, educated at Cambridge, knowledgeable but uneasy in London, full of new and vague aspirations, sought in Puritanism a self-confidence equal to their hopes and became saints on their way, as it were, to becoming governors of new worlds and new societies.

It should be noted that the elective affinity of aristocrats, ministers, gentlemen, merchants, and lawyers with the Calvinist and Puritan ideologies did not lie only in the anxiety they all shared, but also in the *capacity* they all shared to participate in those "exercises" that sainthood required. They were the "sociologically competent"—as has already been argued—they were ready for magistracy and war. The Calvinist faith did not appeal to men, however anxious, below the level of such competence. Laborers and peasants were more likely, if they were free at all from traditional ways, to adopt some more pacific or chiliastic faith whose promise did not depend upon their own hard work, that is, upon the control of themselves and the cruel, unwearying repression of others.

Puritanism cannot, then, be described simply as the ideological reflex of social disorder and personal anxiety; it is one possible response to the experiences of disorder and anxiety, or rather, it is one possible way of perceiving and responding to a set of experiences that other men than the saints might have

viewed in other terms. There were both merchants and gentlemen, for example, who obviously enjoyed the very freedoms that
frightened the saints so much—mobility, extravagance, individual-
ity, and wit—and who eagerly sought out the Renaissance cities
and courts where such freedoms were cultivated. And from
among these new urbanites undoubtedly came many capitalists
and liberals. It would not be easy to explain in particular cases
why the court of James I held such attractions for some members
of the English gentry while it was vicious and iniquitous in the
eyes of others. No more is it readily comprehensible why some
of the newcomers to the burgeoning city of London merged into
the mob or explored the exciting underworld, while others hated
the "wickedness" of the city and sought out virtuous brethren
and a sense of security and confidence in the Puritan congregations. All that can be said is that some of the men living in
this age of social transformation found what was for them a
suitable response in Calvinist ideology. In England, Puritanism
was their effort to capture control of the changing world and
their own lives—hence the insistent concern of the saints with
order, method, and discipline.

The Puritan concern with discipline and order, however, is
not unique in history. Over and over again since the days of the
saints, bands of political radicals have sought anxiously, energeti-
cally, systematically, to transform themselves and their world.
The choice of sainthood, then, need not be described simply as a
reasonable choice for sixteenth and seventeenth-century Englishmen to have made; it can be related systematically to other
choices of other men in similar historical circumstances.

The very appearance of the Puritan saints in English history
suggests the breakdown of an older order in which neither Protestant autodidacts, political exiles, nor voluntary associations of lay
brethren were conceivable. At the same time that breakdown pro-
vides the context within which the choice of sainthood seems
reasonable and appropriate, though not in any individual case
predictable. It is possible to go further than this, however, and
argue that given the breakdown of the old order, it *is* predictable
that some Englishmen would make that reasonable choice. And

further than this: given similar historical circumstances, Frenchmen and Russians would predictably make similar choices. Englishment became Puritans and then godly magistrates, elders and fathers in much the same way and for many of the same reasons as eighteenth-century Frenchmen became Jacobins and active citizens, and twentieth-century Russians Bolsheviks and professional revolutionaries—and then in Lenin's words "leaders," "managers," and "controllers." The Calvinist saints were the first of these bands of revolutionary magistrates who sought above all control and self-control. In different cultural contexts, at different moments in time, sainthood will take on different forms and the saints will act out different revolutions. But the radical's way of seeing and responding to the world will almost certainly be widely shared whenever the experiences which first generated that perception and response are widely shared, whenever groups of men are suddenly set loose from old certainties.

That older order in which Puritanism was unimaginable has been described in the preceding pages as a traditional society, that is, a society in which hierarchy is the fundamental ordering principle; patriarchy, personal loyalty, patronage and corporatism are the key forms of human relations; and passivity is the normal political posture of common men. At some point in the later Middle Ages, the complex institutional structure of European traditionalism began to weaken and erode; its philosophical rationalizations were called into question by bold speculators free, more or less, from traditional controls. Then there began a long period of transition, in which moments of rapid and explosive change alternated with moments of stalemate and frustration. Individual men experienced at once a new and exhilarating sense of freedom and mobility and an acute anxiety and fearfulness, both of which may be summed up in the Puritan notion of "unsettledness." Only gradually, at different times in different countries, did there emerge a new society, whose members were at least formally equal, their political relations impersonal, based either upon negotiation and contract or upon a uniform coercion. In this society the activity of the organized "people" was as necessary to social discipline as was popular passivity in the traditional world. The old order was imagined to be natural and eternal, but it is in the nature of the new that it be regularly renewed. It is the product of art and will, of human doing. If traditionalism was stable, modernity is founded upon change. Even so, however, it represents a routinization of the frenetic mobility that marked the period of transition and of the zeal and anxiety that drove men forward during that exciting and painful time.

The significance of Puritanism lies in the part it played between 1530 and 1660. Those were crucial years of struggle and change in England and those were the years when Calvinism was a forceful, dynamic faith. After the Restoration, its energy was drawn inward, its political aspirations forgotten; the saint gave way to the non-conformist. Or, Lockeian liberalism provided an alternative political outlook. But Puritanism cannot be explained by reference either to its survivals or its transformations; it is necessary to confront the historical reality of those years when it was still an integral creed. In those years, Puritanism provided what may best be called an *ideology of transition*. It was functional to the process of modernization not because it served the purposes of some universal progress, but because it met the human needs that arise whenever traditional controls give way and hierarchical status and corporate privilege are called into question. These needs can be met in other ways: by ideologists of nostalgia, for example, who glorify the old security and the old bondage. But they are met most effectively by doctrines like Puritanism that encourage a vigorous self-control and a narrowing of energies, a bold effort to shape a new personality against the background of social "unsettledness." Once such a personality has been achieved, the saints proceed to shape society in the image of their own salvation; they become what the ideologists of nostalgia can never become: active enemies of the old order. Thus when country gentlemen have experienced a conversion like Cromwell's, they are transformed not only into saints but also into parliamentary intransigents, attacking the traditional hierarchy root and branch and experimenting with new forms of political association.

But though they appear in history as revolutionaries, who destroy the old order and kill the king, the primary source of the saints' radical character lies in their response to the *dis*order of the transition period. The old order is only a part, and not the most important part of their experience. They live much of their lives amidst the breakdown of that order or (as with the clerical intellectuals) in hiding or exile from it. Much as they hated bishops and courtiers, then, the Puritan saints hated and feared vagabonds more and dreaded the consequences of the vagabonds in themselves, their own "unsettledness." "Masterless men" are always the first products of the breakdown of tradition and the saints hardly thought such men less dangerous than did their former masters. Without the experience of masterlessness, the Puritans are unimaginable. Sainthood is one of the likely results of that experience, or rather one of the ways in which men seek to cope with that experience. Hobbist authoritarianism is another way—and the contrast between Hobbes' appeal to sovereign power and the Puritan's struggle for self-control suggests the difficulty of describing sainthood, in Erich Fromm's terms, as an "escape from freedom."

Fromm is certainly right, however, in viewing the saint in the context of "freedom." The Puritans were in no sense the products of a new order slowly growing up within traditional feudal society, as Marxist theory would have it. They were the products —though that word hardly suggests their extraordinary activism— of disorder. They inherited the critical and destructive work of writers like Machiavelli and Luther and they continued that work only after they had organized themselves to survive in the midst of criticism and destruction. They were second-generation men: they arrived in a world where courageous heretics and philosophers had already challenged the traditional masters; they encountered the difficulties of this world by being born again, by rejecting masterlessness and finding a new master in themselves and a new system of control in their godly brethren.

Coping with disorder meant being reborn as a new man, self-confident and free of worry, capable of vigorous, willful activity. The saints sometimes took new names, or gave new names to their children, to signify this rebirth. If the experience of "unsettledness" had made them anxious, depressed, unable to work, given to fantasies of demons, morbid introspection, or fearful daydreams such as Calvin had suggested were common among fallen men, then sainthood was indeed a triumph of character formation. Here the analogy with the Bolsheviks is worth pursuing. Lenin's diatribes against "slovenliness . . . carelessness, untidiness, unpunctuality, nervous haste, the inclination to substitute discussion for action, talk for work, the inclination to undertake everything under the sun without finishing anything" were intended first of all as attacks upon his fellow radicals and exiles—whatever their value as descriptions of the "primitive" Russia he hated so much. The first triumph of Bolshevism, as of Puritanism, was over the impluse toward "disorganization" in its own midst: here, so to speak, was Satan at work where he is ever most active—in the ranks of the godly. It should not be forgotten, however, that this was a triumph also over the impulse toward free thought and spontaneous expression that manifests itself with especial vigor in the period of masterlessness and with which modernity has, up to a point, made its peace. This was the sacrifice which the saints found necessary in their terrible struggle for self-control. The Puritans vigorously attacked Renaissance experimentation in dress and in all the arts of self-decoration and hated the free-wheeling vagabonds who roamed the countryside and crowded into cities, never organizing themselves into families and congregations. They dreaded the dance and the drama, tore down maypoles and closed playhouses; they waged a long, bitter and unending war against fornication. In a similar fashion, the Jacobin leader Robespierre attacked the hedonism and censured the morals of the new bourgeoisie and spitefully connected the radical free thought of the Enlightenment with anti-revolutionary conspiracy. Atheism, he declared, is aristocratic. And again Lenin, preaching with all the energy of a secular Calvinist against free love: "Dissoluteness in sexual life is bourgeois, [it] is a phenomenon of decay. The proletariat is a rising class . . . It needs clarity, clarity and again clarity. And so, I repeat, no weakening, no waste, no destruction of forces."

In fact, Lenin's morality had little to do with the proletariat and the "dissoluteness" he attacked had little to do with the bourgeoisie. He might as well have talked of saints and worldlings as the Puritans did. The contrast he was getting at was between those men who had succumbed to (or taken advantage of!) the disorder of their time—speculators in philosophy, vagabonds in their sexual lives, economic Don Juans—and those who had somehow pulled themselves out of "unsettledness," organized their lives and regained control. The first group were the damned and the second the saved. The primary difference between them was not social, but ideological.

All forms of radical politics make their appearance at moments of rapid and decisive change, moments when customary status is in doubt and character (or "identity") is itself a problem. Before Puritans, Jacobins, or Bolsheviks attempt the creation of a new order, they must create new men. Repression and collective discipline are the typical methods of this creativity: the disordered world is interpreted as a world at war; enemies are discovered and attacked. The saint is a soldier whose battles are fought out in the self before they are fought out in society. Revolution follows from Puritan sainthood—that is, from the triumph over Satanic lusts—and also from Jacobin virtue and from the Bolshevik "steeling" of character; it is the acting out of a new identity, painfully won. This connection between sainthood and revolution is nicely illustrated in John Milton's eulogy of Cromwell: "A commander first over himself; the conqueror of himself, it was over himself he had learnt most to triumph. Hence he went to encounter with an external enemy as a veteran accomplished in all military duties . . ." In traditional societies, this self-conquest is not necessary—except for relatively small numbers of men who for personal reasons choose monasticism as a way of life. In modern societies, it is routine. But there is a point in the modernization process when large numbers of men, suddenly masterless, seek a rigid self-control; when they discover new purposes, dream of a new order, organize their lives for disciplined and methodical activity. These men are prospective saints and citizens; for them Puritanism, Jacobinism, and Bolshevism are appropriate options. At this point in time, they are likely options.

This is not to reduce political radicalism to the psychological therapy of "unsettled" men. The "unsettledness" which Knox, Cartwright, and Cromwell experienced, with all its attendant fearfulness and enthusiasm, sometimes disfiguring and sometimes ennobling, was only a heightened form of the feelings of many of their fellow Englishmen—for ultimately the sociological range of the Puritan response was very wide. Of course, "unsettledness" was not a permanent condition and so sainthood was only a temporary role. The Puritans failed in their effort to transform England into a holy commonwealth and, in one way or another, their more recent counterparts have also failed. Sainthood mediated the dangerous shift from one social routine to another; then it survived only as a remembered enthusiasm and a habitual self-control devoid, as Weber's capitalism is, of theological reason. What this suggests, however, is not that holiness was an impractical dream, the program of neurotic, muddled, or unrealistic men. In fact, Puritan ministers and elders (and fathers) had considerable political experience and the holy commonwealth was in part achieved—among those men who most needed holiness. Nor is it correct to argue from the inability of the saints to retain political power that Puritanism represented only a temporary triumph of "ideas" over "interests" of the holiness doctrine over the ultimately more significant secular purposes of gentlemen, merchants, and lawyers. For what needs to be explained is precisely why the saints over a long period of time acquired such an intense interest in ideas like predestination and holiness. Puritan ideology was a response to real experience, therefore a practical effort to cope with personal and social problems. The disappearance of the militant saints from English politics in the years after the Restoration suggests only that these problems were limited in time to the period of breakdown and psychic and political reconstruction. When men stopped being afraid or became less afraid, then Puritanism was suddenly irrelevant. Particular elements of the Puritan system were transformed to fit the new routine—and other elements were forgotten. And only then did the saint become a man of "good behavior," cautious, respectable, moved only by a routine anxiety and ready to participate in a Lockeian society.

16   Sumner Chilton Powell

The Origin and Stability of a New England Town

*In the last few years there has been a revived interest in the close ex-
amination of small communities in early America. Focusing on particular towns and villages in New England, a few younger historians
have been raising important new questions about social structure, mobility, land holding, patterns of family life, and differences between the
colonies and England. Some of these studies have required the application of highly sophisticated techniques for the analysis of population
statistics. This scholarship is just in its infancy in this country, but
already it has led to some basic questioning of long-held assumptions
about life in the colonies.*

*Unlike some of the other new social historians, Summer Chilton Powell
has made relatively little use of advanced quantitative methods, but his
book on Sudbury, Massachusetts,* Puritan Village: The Formation of a
New England Town, *places the early history of one small group firmly
in the context of American Puritanism. His argument that the founding and development of Sudbury involved fundamental social and institutional innovation has already been both confirmed and challenged by
other studies. The degree and nature of the differences between New
and Old England are now at issue among historians, but there is wide-
spread agreement that the problem can best be explored by the careful
investigation of particular small communities.*

The historical debate on "the origin" of a type of social and
political structure called "the New England town" is probably
not over, but the question itself may be superficial today. We
can now realize that there were multiple origins and many
distinct early towns, and that all of these towns and their re-

SOURCE. Sumner Chilton Powell, "The Origin and Stability of a New England Town" from *Puritan Village: The Formation of a New England Town.*
Garden City, New York: Anchor Books, Doubleday & Company, Inc. 1965, pp.
178–186. Copyright © 1963 by Wesleyan University. Reprinted by permission
of the publisher and author.

lationships need careful examination.

How far back to search for origins was an unsolved dilemma for a previous generation of historians. Charles Andrews was undoubtedly correct when he insisted that there were only superficial likeness between the German *tun,* the Anglo-Saxon village, and the New England town, despite Herbert B. Adams' insistence to the contrary. There are three major difficulties in this whole investigation—the difficulty of finding and transcribing much of the documentary material; the complex interaction between village, regional, and more extensive social, political, and economic structures; and finally, the validity of the search for "the origin." A geneticist can watch the growth of biological structures in controlled experiments and can observe the intricate linkages through hundreds of generations. But the purpose of his experiments is to discover means to eradicate deleterious genes and to improve human genotypes. The purpose of those historians who insisted on the origin of the town has no such clarity.

If the question of the origin seems superficial, the investigation of the change, transition, and stability of English local institutions across the Atlantic ocean in the seventeenth century is not. The members of these groups came from quite diverse social and political locales in England, with definite sets of attitudes and drives, usually expressed in religious terms—but not always. England itself contained a large variety of local institutions. As a skilled archivist and local historian has said, "No place is 'representative' of English local government in seventeenth-century England. The evidence one finds tells us what local government was like in one distinct village, or parish, or town or borough, no more, no less."

Apparently those men and women who emigrated to New England and formed new groups were inventive, as were some who settled in southern areas. Certainly they had the unique challenge of a "town grant," which could be defined more or less as the inhabitants wished.

They made a staggering number of changes. How many men today, founding a "godly plantation" on the moon or on any habitable planet, would make as many significant alterations in religion, in social organization, in local government, and in attitude and values generally? Consider what might be called the constructive dissent in the first generation of Sudbury men. What were the selectmen there actually doing? They were constructing a community of free townsmen. This seems to have been their principal ideal, and their loyalty to the town even transcended their professions of religious faith. They had been trained in a variety of local institutions in England. They knew how to function as jurymen, vestrymen, borough councilors, or parish officers. But they must have wanted more, for they constructed an entirely new type of town.

Even the minister succumbed to the charged atmosphere. When his leadership over the youth was threatened by John Ruddock, when his sermons did not prevent "prophanation of the Lord's Day," he appeared in town meetings and prosecuted his cause "with violence." "Put it to vote!" shouted Edmund Brown. He could not believe that the new political entity would abandon him. But it did—at least for a while. John Ruddock and his group, facing severe restrictions, wanted to construct a new town.

Examine the solemn meetings in Sudbury in January, 1655. Note how completely absent the traditional legal sanctions are. The selectmen did not bolster themselves with citations of Elizabethan laws, English customs, or warrants from local justices of the peace. As far as one can tell from reading the Sudbury orders, the selectmen assumed that once the General Court had made the initial town grant, they were the principal source of power in their area, subject only to the approval of the townsmen. It was very significant that when the General Court sent out an investigating committee in 1656, not only was there resentment in Sudbury, but also there is no indication that the townsmen followed the recommendations on the sizing of the commons.

There seems to have been deep meaning to the phrase in the Sudbury Town Book, *free townsman.* Since it is never fully defined, it may have implied a status more like that of borough freeman than that of freeman written in the orders of the General Court. In Sudbury at any rate, such a man knew he could dissent and that he would be heard.

To quote the town clerk, "John Ruddock, being then present, did, by his vote, dissent from the act." At that point Ruddock was the leader of a minority group. But did he, full of frustration and ill-will, call his youth to arms and resort to violence? He did not. Finding his ambitions blocked in the Musketaquid valley, he proceeded to construct another community. Once again, he rebuilt human institutions in the face of necessity.

Ruddock developed his constructive faith in relation to the area about him and with the full permission and support of the Massachusetts government. When he dissented in 1655, Ruddock hoped that another land area would be available to him and to his petitioners. He could have swallowed his pride and remained in Sudbury. He could have moved across the river and settled on the plots which the selectmen offered him. But he did neither. Whether tacitly or explicitly, he made a series of daring assumptions, involving predictions about his own leadership, his group, the General Court, the Indians, and the opposition party in Sudbury. With his confidence fortified by the grant of town land from the General Court, he then preceeded to express his ideals and his will.

Each step demanded both logic and leadership. Ruddock had to "view" the area to assure his group that it would be productive and satisfying to them. He then recognized the rights of the Indians, although there is no evidence that he tried to communicate with them to see whether they understood his purpose. Had he tried to do this sincerely, he might have made the unhappy discovery that the English concept of the individual, exploitative ownership of soil was causing apprehensions among the original natives.

Next, Ruddock needed to display confidence in his woodsmen and farmers, and to develop this into a reciprocal relationship. Not only did he have to prove that crops could be raised, but he had to show that a market for them could be found and a road built for their transportation. In addition, he had to hope that even though he might be considered immoral, some minister would forgive him and join his new group. This took many years, as the new town later learned.

Above all, Ruddock had to display a type of idealism that

could transcend his previous failures. He probably had to achieve a remarkable synthesis of the new awareness of the ideals of his young followers and his own ability to assist his men in fulfilling them. In short, to be able to establish a community that would function "forever" in the same spot where the leaders planted it, Ruddock must have had a complex mind and a profound faith which he could communicate to others.

Later generations use the term "New England town," and thereby assume the established set of relationships and attitudes which New Englanders have known for decades. Today we think we know what a "town" is. But to the first settlers, the term "town" must have meant a life of uncertainty, balanced by a faith in social order and stability.

To emigrate from accustomed social institutions and relationships to a set of unfamiliar communities in the way in which Noyes and Ruddock shifted from England to Sudbury, and the latter from Sudbury to Marlborough, meant a startling transformation. The townsmen had to change or abandon almost every formal institution which they had taken for granted.

The Sudbury Town Book, read in the context of close examination of English local records of the period, actually describes this set of reforms. The first clerk, Hugh Griffin, began using a new vocabulary as he recorded the orders made by his selectmen and his free townsmen.

Gone were the courts-baron, courts-leet, vestries, out-hundred courts, courts of election, courts of record, courts of the borough, courts of orders and decrees, courts of investigation, courts of ordination, and views of frankpledge. In their place came meetings of men to order town affairs, or later, selectmen's meetings and town meetings, with a few references to the General Court and the county court.

Gone were the seneschal, bailiff, jurymen, virgate, yardland, reversion, messuage, tenement, toft, croft, heriot, close, fealty to the lord, admission, hayward, annual rent, copyholders, coliarholders, and freeholders. In their stead came selectmen, grants of land, freemen, and free townsmen.

The medieval church calendar was completely abandoned in the first generation. Whereas the Hampshire farmers had started the year in England with Lady Day (March 25) and ended it with Plow Monday, which was the first Monday after Epiphany (January 6), the entire calendar in early Sudbury was reduced to a numerical sequence of months, monotonous in their prosaic designations, starting with "the first month" or March. The second generation in both Sudbury and Marlborough returned to the old calendar. The men of Marlborough had a town meeting on December 25, 1663. They were using the day not for the ancient ceremony they had celebrated since childhood, but for a new kind of ritual—the formation of a godly community.

Gone also were the rector, curate, sexton, ringers, glebe land, terrier, tithe, parish perambulation, churchwardens, sidemen, questmen, overseers of the poor, and all the many familiar objects of church "furniture," from the cross to the goblet. The town clerk of Sudbury spoke of pastor, deacon, meetinghouse, town perambulation, and a town "rate" to pay the pastor and to repair or rebuild the meetinghouse.

Into the dark mists had disappeared articles of visitation, Book of Common Prayer, presentments, commissary, archdeacon, church courts, purgation, certificate of penance, and holy days. Hugh Griffin had no substitution for these. As far as local historians can tell, the first Sudbury "church" did not even keep a separate book. Only the visit of the "Reverend Elders" tried to impose an external church discipline on Sudbury, and Griffin did not even record their presence in the Town Book.

Abolished too were the quarter sessions, justices of the peace, knights of the shire, king's sheriff, house of correction, Marshalsea payments, king's bench, assizes, Privy Council, and Parliament. The King and Queen were never mentioned. In their places were governor, magistrates, General Court, and town deputy.

Sudbury was no longer an ancient borough and had no mayor, bailiff, collector of rents of the assizes, chamberlain, chief constable, sergeants at mace, coroner, burgess, aldermen, market overseers, ale tasters, or master of the grammar school. No one met in the Town House or aspired to build paneled rooms for the "select fraternity" who governed the town. They were only selectmen, marshal, clerk, and various townsmen doing various specific jobs, as assigned by the town meeting.

Hugh Griffin did not have to note any maimed soldiers, travelers from Ireland, Dunkirkers, or soldiers from Bohemia. Someone had tried to dignify the resident Indian chiefs by giving them the names Jethro and Cato, but it seems there were few visitors during the first generation, and few people "warned out."

Life in Sudbury was indeed a "new" England. No wonder men like Samuel Gordon and Thomas Morton were amazed and alarmed as they inspected other towns. What held these communities together and gave them stability? What welded relationships and created loyalties and mutual respect?

Bold leaders, the tacit and sometimes actual approval by the General Court, concern for every inhabitant, and a deep faith were sufficient for the first generation of Sudbury townsmen. One can argue that three institutions gave a structure and a harmony to the community: the open-field system of farming, the town meeting, and the town church. Sudbury continued "general and particular" fields until 1694, and Professor Ault has clearly shown how this joint administration of agriculture led to a kind of local democratic government. The Sudbury town meeting considered a wide variety of social problems, from the granting, renting, taxation, and sale of land to bastardy and the mental health of its citizens. When one reads the Town Book closely, one is impressed that the selectmen were aware of the precise "condition" of every inhabitant and quick to note any "dangerous" or "suspicious" person amongst the group. Any unusual occurrence which caused a problem seems to have been brought before the town, and the townsmen voted on the policy of warning out "maimed, defective, or suspicious persons," the problem of finding a smith and keeping the mill running, the correct height of field fences, an inventory of "all mens' estates," and the sickness of any citizen. They also considered the menace of hungry crows and marauding wolves, the correct placement of roads between communities, and any infringement of town meadow or town land, which seems to have been managed as a kind of corporate bank account, to be granted, rented, or called back at the will of the inhabitants and selectmen.

The Sudbury church seems to have been virtually indistinguishable from the town throughout the seventeenth century, but it must have given a sense of order and security until 1655, after which the church was "in a most deplorable state, from which it was long in recovering." Town meetings discussed the problem of finding a substitute when the Reverend Edmund Brown fell ill in 1678, hired his successor, the Reverend James Sherman, and set the conditions of his contract, drew up the design and levied taxes for the third meetinghouse 1686–1688, appealed to those citizens who were negligent in paying their share of Mr. Sherman's salary, and decided who could or could not build pews in the church in place of the normal "seats left open at both ends."

The first generation found that it could not abandon the traditional calendar, and from 1648 onward the pagan names of February, March, and the rest were introduced into the Town Book and have been used ever since. The second generation, however, returned to several deep-seated English institutions and customs. The farmers grew "English pasture" and sedge fences, the military company purchased a "flight of colors," men were elected tithingmen to collect the church tax, and town accounts began to appear in the Town Book, making some pages read like any English borough book, citing income and expenses.

The most significant institution which was reintroduced was the English common law. When Widow Loker refused to resign to the town the housing, ground, trees, and privileges which she had sold to the town, the selectmen turned to the county court at Cambridge and started a suit at law. Another entry indicates the relationship of Sudbury to the courts and to ultimate authority. "This day Sarjt. Barnard made report to the Town what success hee mett withall att the Quarter Sessions; and then did chuse a commity to meet with and treat the Jury that shall be appointed to state his Majesties hy way betweene our Town and Marlbrough and Indevor to the uttmost of thear power that it may bee layd out so as it may bee last prejudijuall to our Town."

Ten years before Barnard's report, Sudbury acknowledged that it was now part of the British empire, for the town, desiring to be rid of one D. Hedley, warned him out in "his Majesty's name." The King's tax started to be collected by the town constable by

April, 1693, and once again these town officers relied on the ultimate authority of the King. It is particularly interesting to read that the town voted a special tax of "eight pounds in money . . . for the sending and transporting of Thomas Blake to Old England." The absence of any references in the Sudbury Town Book to "his Majesty" during the famous governorship of Sir Edmund Andros, 1686–1690, clearly illustrates the spirit of insubordination of which the governor constantly complained while he was in Boston. Apparently Sudbury was willing to acknowledge the authority of the King, but on its own terms and at specific times.

Sudbury, like the other early New England towns, was a remarkable experiment in the formation and growth of a social community. Now that this town presents an explicit case study, further examination in group behavior can be made of the whole problem of the growth and stability of such communities, provided that accurate categories of investigation are formed. William Caudill suggests the concepts of the "stress" on various groups and the formation of "linked open systems" and feels that students should consider the Atlantic only as a highway between related communities. He advises that we try to define and discover "cultural pairs" of communities on both sides of the ocean and then ask why some citizens left, why some stayed, why some shuttled back and forth in the whole Atlantic system. Bernard Bailyn has clearly shown that the Boston merchants returned to the British trade system by the end of the seventeenth century, and certainly both the inhabitants and the free townsmen of Sudbury felt the compelling need of the authority of the King and common law by the second generation.

If, as it seems, we today are in a period of radical social upheaval and violent transformation of communities and entire national and international populations, much perspective can be gained from close examination of a somewhat analogous period in the seventeenth century. Above all, we should not lose the faith in our ability to create "godly, orderly communities," or our desire to rely on law and common consent, rather than on violence and the authority of a powerful central government. If we abandon our New England heritage, we do so at our peril.

The Sudbury townsmen might not have been able to order their community "forever" as they hoped, but they set a remarkable example for all the generations which have followed them.

SUGGESTED READING

This highly selective bibliography does not include the works from which selections have been taken for this reader. Titles with asterisks are available in paperback editions.

MODERN EDITIONS OF PRIMARY SOURCES

*Miller, Perry, and Thomas H. Johnson, eds., *The Puritans: A Source Book of Their Writings*, rev. ed.; 2 vols. New York: Harper & Row, 1963.) The best, most comprehensive, easily available collection of writings by the American Puritans, with an excellent introduction and extensive bibliography.)

Winthrop, John, *Journal, History of New England, 1630–1649*, J. K. Hosmer, ed. New York: Barnes & Noble, 1908. (The single most important source for the early history of Massachusetts.)

ENGLISH PURITANISM

George, Charles, and Katherine George, *The Protestant Mind of the English, Reformation, 1570–1640*. Princeton: Princeton University Press, 1961. (A major, controversial study of English religious history which minimizes the theological differences between Anglicans and Puritans.)

* Haller, William, *The Rise of Puritanism: Or, The Way to the New Jerusalem as Set Forth in Pulpit and Press from Thomas Cartwright to John Lilburne and John Milton, 1570–1643*. New York: Harper & Row, 1957. (The study of English Puritanism should begin with this excellent book.)

New, John F., *Anglican and Puritan: The Basis of Their Opposition, 1558–1640*. Stanford: Stanford University Press, 1964. (A brief, intensive study of the deeper theological issues that divided Anglicans and Puritans.)

*Simpson, Allan, *Puritanism in Old and New England*. Chicago: The University of Chicago Press, 1961. (A brief, well-written book that attempts some generalizations about the significance of Puritanism through an examination of several features of its history in both England and America.)

Trinterud, Leonard J., "The Origins of Puritanism," *Church History*, XX, No. 1, 37–57 (1951). (An important study of the earliest development of English Puritanism that emphasizes the non-Calvinist roots of the covenant theology.)

POLITICAL AND SOCIAL HISTORY OF NEW ENGLAND

*Bailyn, Bernard, *Education in the Formation of American Society*. New York: Random House, 1960. (A brief, highly original study that relates the early development of education in the American colonies, including New England, to the history of the family in terms of institutional innovation.)

Brown, B. Katherine, "Freemanship in Puritan Massachusetts," *American Historical Review*, LIX, 865–883 (July 1954). (Argues that early Massachusetts was more democratic than previously had been thought.)

Demos, John, "Families in Colonial Bristol, Rhode Island: An Exercise in Historical Demography," *The William and Mary Quarterly*, 3d ser., XXV, 40–57 (January 1968). (A study of great methodological significance that undermines many common scholarly assumptions about family life in early New England.)

*Erikson, Kai F., *Wayward Puritans: A Study in the Sociology of Deviance*. New York: John Wiley and Sons, 1966. (A sociologically oriented study of atypical and antisocial behavior, this book raises important questions about changes in the American Puritans' conception of their community.)

Forster, Stephen, "The Massachusetts Franchise in the Seventeenth Century," *The William and Mary Quarterly*, 3d ser., XXIV, 613–623 (October 1967). (Probes the evidence used to support the argument that early Massachusetts was relatively democratic and indicates some of the difficulties of constructing a reliable estimate of the extent of the franchise.)

Haskins, George Lee, *Law and Authority in Early Massachusetts: A Study in Tradition and Design*. Hamden, Connecticut: Shoe String Press, 1968. (The development of law seen in the context of intellectual and social history.)

Lockridge, Kenneth, "Land, Population and the Evolution of New England Society, 1630–1670," *Past and Present*, No. 39, 62–80 (April 1968). (An excellent example of the new demographic history which may overturn some of our basic assumptions about the social development of early New England.)

*Morgan, Edmund S., *The Puritan Dilemma: The Story of John Winthrop*. Boston: Little, Brown, 1958. (This short, highly readable biography of the first governor of the Bay Colony succeeds in humanizing the founders of New England. It is probably the best starting point for the beginning student of American Puritanism.)

*———, *The Puritan Family: Religion and Domestic Relations in Seventeenth Century New England*, rev. ed. New York: Harper & Row, 1966. (A pioneering work full of suggestive insights. Still of great importance in spite of the questions that have been raised about some of its conclusions by the new demographic historians.)

*Morison, Samuel Eliot, *Builders of the Bay Colony*, rev. ed. Boston: Houghton Mifflin, 1963. (A history of early Massachusetts presented in biographical accounts of some of its leaders.)

RELIGIOUS HISTORY OF AMERICAN PURITANISM

Battis, Emery, *Saints and Sectaries: Anne Hutchinson and the Antinomian Controversy in the Massachusetts Bay Colony*. Chapel Hill: The University of North Carolina Press for The Institute of Early American History and Culture, 1962. (An account of the great turmoil caused by the Antinomian heresy, with a sociological analysis of its roots.)

*Miller, Perry, *From Colony to Province*, Vol. II of *The New England Mind*. Boston: Beacon Press, 1961. (A brilliant history of the development of the religious ideas of the American Puritans in the context of the social and political history of seventeenth-century New England. It is based in part on the framework laid out in *The New England Mind: The Seventeenth Century*, although it can be read profitably apart from its companion volume.)

———, *Orthodoxy in Massachusetts*. Cambridge: Harvard University Press, 1933. (Miller's first book describes the development of nonseparating Congregationalism in England and its establishment as the religion of New England.)

*Morgan, Edmund S., *Visible Saints: The History of a Puritan Idea*. New York: New York University Press, 1963. (A careful study of the development of the method of determining eligibility for membership in the New England churches by testing candidates for indications of grace.)

Ong, Walter J., "The Lady and the Issue," in *In the Human Grain: Further Explorations of Contemporary Culture,* pp. 188–202. New York: The Macmillan Co., 1967. (By a leading Jesuit scholar. A psychoanalytically oriented discussion of the rejection of women implicit in Protestantism and Puritanism with important implications for American culture in general. Highly controversial, but very interesting.)

Pettit, Norman, *The Heart Prepared: Grace and Conversion in Puritan Spiritual Life.* New Haven: Yale University Press, 1966. (A close study of the development of some important Puritan ideas regarding salvation which shows particular sensitivity to the emotional factors in religion.)

*Starkey, Marion, *The Devil in Massachusetts: A Modern Inquiry into the Salem Witch Trials.* New York: Doubleday & Co. (A well-written account of the Salem witch scare with some suggestions about its psychological roots.)

PURITANISM AND "MODERNISM"

*Hill, Christopher, *Society and Puritanism in Pre-Revolutionary England.* New York: Schocken Books, 1964. (The most important book by the leading Marxist historian of seventeenth-century England. Presents a wealth of information to support the view that there was a positive correlation between Puritanism and the forces of modernization.)

*Tawney, R. H., *Religion and the Rise of Capitalism.* New York: The New American Library, 1947. (The classic Marxist study of the relationship between Protestantism and capitalism which argues that economic factors were the ultimate cause of the changes in the early modern period.)

Trevor-Roper, Hugh Redwald, *The Crisis of the Seventeenth Century: Religion, the Reformation, and Social Change.* New York: Harper & Row, 1968. (A collection of penetrating essays places the history of English Puritanism in the context of contemporary continental events. Trevor-Roper attacks the idea of a positive relationship between Protestantism and capitalism and questions the modernity of the Puritans.)

*Weber, Max, *The Protestant Ethic and the Spirit of Capitalism.* New York: Charles Scribner's Sons, 1930. (This sociological classic argues that Protestantism prepared men for capitalistic activity. The debate over the relationship between religion and economic life in the sixteenth and seventeenth centuries began with this book.)

HISTORIOGRAPHY

Greven, Phillip J., Jr., "Historical Demography and Colonial America," *The William and Mary Quarterly*, 3d ser., XXIV, 438–454 (July 1967). (A review of several of the basic European works in demographic history with important suggestions for the application of these methods to early American history.)

Hollinger, David A., "Perry Miller and Philosophical History." *History and Theory*, VII, 189–202 (1968). (A penetrating analysis of Miller's methods and assumptions focusing on his use of the concept of "tension" to illuminate cultural history.)

Morgan, Edmund S., "Historians of Early New England," in *The Reinterpretation of Early American History*, pp. 41–63, Ray Billington, ed. San Marino, California: The Huntington Library, 1966. (An extremely helpful survey of the history of writings on the Puritan colonies.)

Solt, Leo, "Puritanism, Capitalism, Democracy and the New Science." *American Historical Review*, LXXIII, 18–29 (October 1967). (A discussion of a large number of works on various aspects of the relation between Puritanism and modernism by a historian of seventeenth-century England who is skeptical about that relationship.)

Wise, Gene, "Implicit Irony in Recent American Historiography: Perry Miller's New England Mind." *Journal of the History of Ideas*, XXIV, 579–600 (October-December 1968). (A brillian study of the most important historian of American Puritanism with some significant suggestions regarding the implications of Miller's work in the study of American history in general.)